Why I Still Believe the Gospel

Why I Still Believe the Gospel

Clarence Boomsma

With a foreword by

Andrew Kuyvenhoven

WILLIAM B. EERDMANS PUBLISHING COMPANY

GRAND RAPIDS, MICHIGAN / CAMBRIDGE, U.K.

Wm. B. Eerdmans Publishing Co.

2140 Oak Industrial Drive N.E., Grand Rapids, Michigan 49505 /
P.O. Box 163, Cambridge CB3 9PU U.K.

Printed in the United States of America

12 11 10 09 08 07   7 6 5 4 3 2 1

Library of Congress Cataloging-in-Publication Data

Boomsma, Clarence.
Why I still believe the Gospel / Clarence Boomsma;
With a foreword by Andrew Kuyvenhoven.
p.   cm.
Includes bibliographical references.
ISBN 978-0-8028-2736-4 (pbk.: alk. paper)
1. Apologetics.   I. Title.

BT1103.B65   2007

239 — dc22

2007009967

www.eerdmans.com

To my parents,

Bert and Jennie Boomsma,

with gratitude to God for the

faith, hope, and love

they modelled

Contents

—⟨⟨⟨⟨⟩⟩⟩⟩—

Foreword

=⊸⊘⊘⊘⊶=

The validity of Christian faith and action depends on the reality of the resurrection of Jesus of Nazareth. The whole picture hangs on that one nail. If Jesus is dead, we are fooling each other and wasting our time. But if he returned from death to life, the world has changed direction and human life can never be the same again.

Christians believe that Jesus lives and that Christ is Lord. But all of us have shivers of doubt and suffer attacks and temptations. We know, of course, that wherever faith is, there is also doubt. But although faith and doubt co-exist, they are no friends. They are enemies, and either one must win the battle.

Clarence Boomsma has kept the faith. In this monograph he leaves us his testimony. Many will be comforted already by the fact that he, even he, writes about My Crisis of Faith. For Boomsma has been a leader among a generation of pastors in the Christian Reformed Church in North America. They know him as a diligent pastor of a large congregation who was also a widely involved churchman. His personal faith, pastoral devotion, and theological judgment made him a paradigm. Ecclesiastical boards and assemblies often chose him as their president. But he was most useful to — and beloved by — countless people as a preacher of the gospel of Christ. During his entire ministry he was fuelled by a voracious reading habit. As a matter of fact, when you read all his references to theologians and philosophers, you would almost forget that this man was not an academician but a busy pastor.

This little book is Boomsma's defense of the reasonableness of the Christian faith in our "enlightened" age. He has been formulating this defense all along, though he only started to write it down when he retired. For him the Easter event is not only the lynchpin of the Christian faith, as it is for all of us; it is also the strategic point in our defense of the gospel. For Boomsma Christ's resurrection is the only adequate explanation of the existence of the church (and of the New Testament canon). It is the window through which we know God himself and what his plans are for the human race. Thus the book is not only a boost to all of us who have faith, but also a real challenge to naturalists. Boomsma has seen the rise and fall of arrogant theological liberalism, and he is no stranger to the current imperialism of the scientific method that accepts no phenomenon that it cannot explain by its own limited methods. And he asks them: "What do you think of Jesus Christ, risen from death?"

In our new century, some import religiosity from East Asia, and all of us in North America have to come to terms with a fierce Muslim faith. Therefore we ought to concentrate on the utterly unique feature of our faith: We believe a living Savior! The dead might be remembered and revered. But the living cross our paths.

ANDREW KUYVENHOVEN

Acknowledgments

———❧❧❧———

I have long hesitated to give this exposure to the faith and doubts that have characterized my life as a pastor. I do so now in the hope that it may help others in their struggle with the Christian faith. I acknowledge my debt to David and Lorrie Vander Ark, who not only encouraged the writing of this testimony but also assisted with the early stages of its publication. I am also grateful for friends who urged me to consider its wider distribution, especially Dr. Richard Wevers and my distinguished classmate, Dr. John William Wevers, for their support. Most of all, I am deeply grateful to my wife, Shirley, who gave the support I needed to complete this manuscript.

CLARENCE BOOMSMA

My Crisis of Faith

———≈✺✺✺≈———

When I retired after serving forty years in the gospel ministry, I ended my farewell remarks to my fellow pastors by
affirming that I still believed the gospel I had preached and
taught all those years. That confession was rooted in my personal
pilgrimage of faith and doubt through a lifetime in which I faced
the powerful challenges of unbelief from the modern world and
wrestled with its monumental assaults on the Christian faith.

By saying that I *still* believed I was recalling a crucial and poi-
gnant crisis that shook me deeply shortly after I entered the ministry four decades earlier. I had asked myself haunting questions
after reading two books that severely challenged my faith and the
legitimacy of my ministry: Can I in honesty and with personal integrity continue to believe and preach the gospel? At the end of
my ministry what will my confession be? Will I *still* believe the
gospel?

The first book was the classic work of Albert Schweitzer entitled *The Quest of the Historical Jesus.*[1] It had been a reading assignment in a New Testament course in the seminary, but at the time I
read it fast and uncritically under the pressure of my other studies

1. London: A. & C. Black, 1906.

and a demanding extracurricular workload. But I recognized it as a book of defining importance and resolved to read it more carefully when I was in the ministry. So, soon after settling in my first congregation, I reread this masterful survey of the history of the critical investigation of the life of Jesus that had begun one hundred and fifty years earlier with scholars committed to the secular values of the Enlightenment. The book culminates with Schweitzer's own contribution to the quest, in which he characterizes Jesus as a man obsessed with the immediacy of the coming kingdom of God by divine intervention through himself as God's Messiah. Schweitzer concludes with the bleak and tragic picture of Jesus in his crucifixion, finally surrendering his faith and vision in defeat and despair as witnessed in his awful cry of dereliction: "My God, my God, why hast thou forsaken me?" Schweitzer continues, "At midday of the same day — it was the 14th Nisan, and in the evening the Paschal lamb would be eaten — Jesus cried aloud and expired. He had chosen to remain fully conscious to the last" (p. 395). For Schweitzer there was no resurrection. He apparently deemed the resurrection so obviously impossible for modern-day readers to believe that he felt no need to argue the point.

Nonetheless he describes the life and death of Jesus in terms of cosmic heroism:

> Jesus, in the knowledge that he is the coming Son of Man, lays hold of the wheel of the world to set it moving on that last revolution which is to bring all ordinary history to a close. It refuses to turn, and he throws himself upon it. Then it does turn; and crushes him. Instead of bringing in the eschatological conditions, he has destroyed them. The wheel rolls onward, and the mangled body of one immeasurably great man, who was strong enough to think of himself as the spiritual ruler of mankind as to bend history to his purposes, is hanging upon it still. That is his victory and his reign. (p. 368)

Schweitzer defines what is significant about Jesus for us:

> We must be prepared to find that the historical knowledge
> of the personality and life of Jesus will not be a help, but per-
> haps even an offense to religion. But the truth is, it is not Je-
> sus as historically known, but Jesus as spiritually arisen
> within men, who is significant for our time and can help it.
> Not the historical Jesus, but the spirit which goes forth from
> Him and in the spirits of men strives for new influence and
> rule, is that which overcomes the world.
>
> It is not given to history to disengage that which is abid-
> ing and eternal in the being of Jesus from the historical
> forms in which it worked itself out, and to introduce it into
> our world as a living influence. . . . The abiding and eternal
> in Jesus is absolutely independent of historical knowledge
> and can only be understood by contact with His spirit which
> is still at work in the world. In proportion as we have the
> Spirit of Jesus we have the true knowledge of Jesus. Jesus as a
> concrete historical personality remains a stranger to our
> time, but His spirit, which lies hidden in His words, is known
> in simplicity, and its influence is direct. Every saying con-
> tains in its own way the whole Jesus. (p. 399)

Schweitzer concludes his *Quest of the Historical Jesus* with a
mystical rhapsody that reflects his own faith in the spirit of Jesus
that moved him to his noble and sacrificial career of mercy in the
primitive jungles of Africa:

> He comes to us as One unknown, without a name, as of old,
> by the lake-side, He came to those men who knew Him not.
> He speaks to us the same word: "Follow thou me!" and sets
> us to the tasks which He has to fulfill for our time. He com-
> mands. And to those who obey Him, whether they be wise
> or simple, He will reveal Himself in the toils, the conflicts,

the sufferings which they shall pass through in His fellowship, and, as an ineffable mystery, they shall learn in their own experience Who He is. (p. 401)

The book is a complete dismissal of the New Testament portrayal of Jesus, as the incarnate Son of God who by his life, sufferings, death and resurrection is the Savior and Lord of the world. To accept Schweitzer's reading of the Gospels was to reject totally what C. S. Lewis called the "mere Christianity"[2] at the core of the church's message for nineteen hundred years. Even his sympathetic biographer, Werner Picht,[3] admits it is not easy to know what to make of Schweitzer's intellectual and spiritual position: "Is it still possible to call it Christian?" (p. 12). I was convinced that if Schweitzer was right, nothing remained of my understanding of the gospel that I could preach, teach, or believe. And from what I could make of his concluding statements, I found no gospel there, either. However admirable the dedicated and surrendered life of Albert Schweitzer in the jungles of Africa, it was not based on the faith that the church had confessed and proclaimed through the centuries but on his version of the "Christ of Faith" that arose in the church after the life and death of the "Jesus of History." Schweitzer does not address the perplexing mystery and apparent absurdity of how what amounted to the lunacy and tragedy of the Jesus of History could give rise to the noble and exemplary Christ of Faith that inspired the world's greatest religion to come into being.

It was in this troubled state of mind that I read a second book that had been given to me during my seminary years but that I had not read: *Confessions of an Old Priest*, published in 1922,[4] some twenty years before my ordination in 1943. The author, S. D.

2. *Mere Christianity* (New York: Harper and Row, 1964).
3. *The Life and Thought of Albert Schweitzer* (New York: Harper and Row, 1965).
4. New York: Macmillan, 1922.

4

McConnell, an Episcopalian I believe, published a book after his retirement explaining why he no longer believed what he had proclaimed for fifty years. He had begun his ministry as an orthodox, Bible-believing Christian from a Scottish Presbyterian background who accepted the Christian faith as taught through the centuries. But during his years in the service of the church he had become progressively more liberal in his views, though he had chosen not to make public how his mind was changing. By the time of his retirement he had become what was called in those days a thoroughgoing modernist. He no longer believed that Jesus Christ was the unique, divine Son of God, nor that the church was rooted in a divine revelation. He had not shared his growing unbelief while active in the ministry, but upon retiring he felt compelled to explain the steps and stages that led to the complete collapse of his faith in the classic formulations of Christian belief.

McConnell summarizes his rejection of the alleged factual foundation of the Christian faith:

> The alleged facts are the foundation upon which it [Christianity] is founded; — that Jesus was conceived of the Holy Ghost, born of a virgin, died and was buried and rose again and ascended into heaven from whence he rules the universe. If these be not factual realities belief in the Incarnation, the Atonement, the Judgment by the Son of Man are but silly imaginings. When I first began to be uneasy in the presence of these dogmas, when I began to realize that they were out of all relation to intellectual integrity, to ethical values, to the fact of human experience, I consoled myself with the thought that they were illegitimate conclusions from the accepted life and teaching of Christ. Further reflection convinced me that if the Jesus of the New Testament was, and did and said the things he is represented to have done, the dogmatic conclusions are not only legitimate but inevitable. They are the only interpretations possible of

such a life. No phenomena in the whole history of the race or conceivable by the mind of man can equal these facts if they be facts. They transcend all events, all discoveries. We are dulled to their significance by their constant iteration. Is it a fact that in the whole history of the race one man child and one only named Jesus was born of a virgin mother? Did he speak words of such supernal knowledge as would be impossible for any man? Did he by a word heal lepers, restore palsied limbs, give sight to those born blind? Did he raise dead men from the grave? Did he rise again from the tomb himself? Did he? Unless these be veritable occurrences, in the same sense as the assassination of Julius Caesar, the overwhelming of Pompeii or the conquests of Alexander, the sanction and obligation of Christianity disappears. If, on the other hand, they be real historical events, then all the claims and conclusions of theological dogma and all the statements of the Creeds are too little rather than too much. In that case, exaggeration is impossible. If the facts are so, the *Trisagion* and *Te Deum* are all too feeble. But devotion and worship must wait in silence until the question of fact is determined. Surely phenomena of such transcendent import demand commensurate evidence. Just what is the evidence for the statements concerning Jesus Christ contained in the Creeds? (pp. 13-14)

McConnell found no credible evidence, and he acknowledged that the *Zeitgeist* of the Enlightenment had molded him unconsciously so that he had come to dismiss all miracles, including the resurrection, as being not only "intellectually incredible, but that belief in them was ethically debauching. . . . I have become convinced that miracles do not happen, never have happened, and ought not to happen" (p. 30). Nowhere does he explicitly deal with the resurrection of Jesus, but merely includes it in catalogues of biblical miracles he does not believe.

McConnell's book was for me a shattering attack on and rejection of all the fundamentals of the Christian faith, similar to my own, that the author once believed but had discarded in the light of the natural and social sciences, the historical, scientific criticism of the Bible, and the encounter with the dogmas and beliefs of other world religions. I found McConnell's *Confessions* particularly disturbing because they pinpointed and addressed many of my unanswered questions and confronted boldly the doubts of which I was aware but had tabled and ignored in my own mind.

These two provocative books were a severe challenge for which I had no reasonable reply. My seminary training had not prepared me for, nor seriously addressed, such monumental assaults on the fundamentals of the Christian faith. But these secularizing conceits, I knew, were shaping, permeating, and dominating the entire educated world, leaving little room for the truth of Christianity and its relevance for modern life. Schweitzer and McConnell were both inheritors of "the clash between belief in revelation and scientific thought when the latter presented itself as the sole champion of truth, and decided that it was possible to detect what is 'true' from what is 'untrue' by means of scientific criteria; in other words, when it decided that truth can be discovered by the scientific method."[5]

Shortly into the first year of my ministry I had a disturbing visit with a college classmate and friend who was teaching psychology at the University of Michigan. He asked me, with a touch of sadness and concern, if I was aware that the biblical, orthodox faith of our church that we had been taught at our denominational college was totally rejected and completely ignored by the faculties of the university. Orthodox Christianity simply had no respect or credibility on the university campus. The dominance of science outlawed any role for the supernatural in any area of life. I knew that after the modernist/Fundamentalist controversies of

5. Picht, *Albert Schweitzer*, p. 203.

the 1920s orthodox Christianity had faded from the screen of the media as a dying, discredited subculture that deserved to be ignored. Any religious news that was still reported always involved the bigger churches of the liberal, mainline denominations.

Even though the clash of modernism with orthodoxy was still a live issue in many churches, my seminary training dealt with it only tangentially. It was not, I believe, that my seminary professors were unaware of the strife between the gospel and modernism. I do recall that Professor D. H. Kromminga, one of my favorite teachers, believed the cleavage between orthodoxy and modernism to be so radical and fundamental that the chasm between them was unbridgeable and that each camp might as well go its own way without pursuing a resolution of their differences. The history of the past half-century had largely demonstrated the accuracy of Kromminga's assessment. The fact is that Fundamentalism, no longer on the radar screen of the media, went its own way. It continued to grow in expanding numbers in the latter half of the twentieth century, and part of it evolved into an evangelicalism that gained more intellectual and learned respectability in the world at large. Today evangelicalism has the attention of the media and is much in the news as a more dominant force in American society and politics than the old mainline liberal churches. Numerous conservative seminaries are crowded with thousands of students who go on to occupy pulpits and build megachurches throughout the country. Meanwhile, the fortunes of liberalism have come upon hard times in mainline churches and institutions. Union Theological Seminary in New York City, which in the 1950s was a leading bastion of theological liberalism with more than 700 students, now advertises in *The Christian Century* that it has rooms to let for visitors to New York City. Each camp — orthodoxy and modernism — has gone its own way without any significant rapprochement. Today the clash in religion is primarily between secularism and evangelicalism both within and outside the old mainline churches.

While Schweitzer's and McConnell's books precipitated an existential crisis of faith at the very beginning of my ministry, they were not my first encounter with the powerful assaults that undermine and destroy the faith of so many people reared in the church. I have always had an inquisitive mind, and already in junior high school I was introduced to the challenge that modern science poses for the Bible, with its discovery of the immensity of space and eons of time and particularly its evolutionary hypothesis of the world's origins. Later, on a street corner in Grand Rapids one Sunday evening, I spoke with a man, either a Hindu or Muslim, who caustically derided me and Christians for maintaining Christianity as the only true religion. It was my first encounter with the challenge of other religions that has intensified as the world has increasingly shrunk through modern communication and transportation. While canvassing on behalf of my home church in Indiana I met an older man, an atheist, who was very certain and vocal that there was nothing to all that "Christian stuff" on the basis of his own experience. I was embarrassed at the time because I did not know how to respond to his confident rejection of my beliefs. Beginning in high school and continuing in college I learned from my history, science, and philosophy courses and textbooks how dominant were the naturalistic perspectives of modern life that had no need for God or room for the supernatural anywhere. In the seminary I gained little more than an awareness of "higher biblical criticism" that called the divine inspiration and reliability of the Scriptures into question. Such was my earlier exposure to the powerful challenges directed against my orthodox understanding of the Christian faith. My experience is probably typical of many students reared in Christian homes that bifurcates them with an unresolved tension between their secular education and their Christian faith.

What the reading of Schweitzer and McConnell did was to bring the full impact of these assaults into sharper focus with a devastating critique of my faith, for which I lacked the resources to reply. What could I do in my unsettled, threatened, and lonely state of mind as a young pastor? I was not ready to surrender the faith that I believed from my earliest youth, which gave meaning and purpose, values and goals, directions and commitments, comfort and hope to my life. My faith meant assent to the teachings of the church based on the Holy Scriptures that center in the Jesus of history who became the living Christ of faith through his death and resurrection. I believed him to be my Savior from sin in this sin-saturated world of which I was so much a part and in which I confessed him to be the Lord of my life. But my faith was more than assent to the truths of the Christian faith: I believed myself to be experientially and mysteriously joined to Christ, whom for all practical purposes I equated with God. It was a union that elicited my response of trust, understanding, obedience, hope, and love, even though to my constant regret I continued daily to carry much of the baggage of my sinful heritage that betrayed my allegiance. I considered my union with Christ similar to an intimate person-to-person relationship. It meant commitment to and cultivation of the sense of Christ's presence. Because he is physically absent I believed that such fellowship with Christ required continual cultivation by means of Word and sacrament, prayer and spiritual fellowship with fellow believers. These means aroused and deepened within me the sense of the holy presence of the Triune God. Schweitzer and McConnell challenged the reality of my faith by denying the biblical message that the Jesus of history and the Christ of faith are one and the same through the miracle of the resurrection. These books, if true, meant discounting my religious experience to mere psychological conditioning through family nurture and example, church teaching, worship and fellowship, a strong, cohesive support group, and my own resolve to believe.

I was not ready to surrender my faith commitment without a serious struggle. Nor was I prepared to quit the ministry I had just begun and to which I believed I was called since the days of my earliest recollection and for which I had spent seven years in preparation in college and seminary. At the same time I knew I could not be a dishonest minister, a hypocrite in the pulpit, preaching and teaching what I did not and could not believe was true. I could not follow what seemed to be McConnell's duplicity in the ministry. I was in an agonizing bind. Having once confronted these stark, fundamental, and powerful challenges to my beliefs, I could not disregard them and still live with integrity. I spent several agonizing days and fitful nights in the old parsonage wrestling with these challenges.

But then I remembered two simple, common-sense considerations that had stood me in good stead during my high school and college years when confronted with unsettling questions and doubts about the faith. The first was to recognize and acknowledge that I could not ignore these challenges; as a Christian I had to be intellectually honest whatever the cost. It was better to be an honest doubter than a dishonest believer. I had to accept the challenge that radical criticism of my faith demanded. I knew it would require hard study, serious research, and profound reflection, possibly for years, either to find satisfactory answers to the doubts that now haunted my mind or to modify my understanding of the gospel, however revolutionary that modification might be. I could not imagine a complete rejection of my Christian faith — as apparently neither could Albert Schweitzer. This consideration meant postponing any major decisions for the time being. Secondly — and this seemed most reasonable and most helpful — it was only fair to postpone any conclusions or make any decisions that called into question my Christian faith until I had learned what the responses of intelligent and learned fellow believers were to these fundamental criticisms. After all, I was not the first person to wrestle with the challenges of reconciling science and the Bible, or the critique of philosophical agnosticism, or the higher criticism that undermined the veracity and authority of the Bible, or the uncertainty and diversity of the human experience of God in diverse religions. It seemed only fair as a believer to draw on the resources of "the communion of the saints." Through the years I have cautioned myself repeatedly with these two guidelines to refrain from drawing hasty conclusions and making radical decisions.

There were two options open to me to learn more about the issues involved. One immediate option was to read the books that I already possessed in my library that were relevant to my concerns. The second was to interact with fellow believers and critics that would help me explore the issues and learn of proposed solutions that were lacking in my seminary training. Not that the seminary should have apologized for such lacking: at the time the denomination the seminary was intended to serve was so insulated and separated from the world of modern thought that an education adapted to do battle with modern thinking would have been an irrelevant curriculum in the judgment of most of the students. In my circumstances my immediate options were limited by my commitment to my congregation, by my lack of financial resources for graduate study, and by the lack of an institution of higher learning nearby for advanced part-time study. I had been advised to do graduate work at Princeton Theological Seminary upon graduation from the seminary and in fact had been accepted to pursue a master's degree, but with the shortages of ministers during World War II, I chose rather to serve a congregation with the thought of pursuing graduate study after a few years in the ministry once the war was over.

Meanwhile, in the summer of 1945, I attended the two-week sessions of the second Princeton Institute of Theology. There the wisdom of my holding all decisions in abeyance was particularly reinforced when I heard Dr. Harris Read, one of the lecturers, a respected scholar and pastor of a downtown Presbyterian Church in Baltimore, relate in an informal setting with conferees how as a young man he had read Albert Schweitzer's *Quest* and had been greatly disturbed by it. I interrupted to ask how he had dealt with the challenge of the *Quest*. I no longer remember his answer, but at the time, I recall, it seemed an adequate reply to assure me that Schweitzer's position was vulnerable and by no means the last word. I went home reassured that I had made the right decision not to make any hasty decisions regarding my beliefs or my ministry.

My professor of theology, Louis Berkhof, made frequent references in class to Karl Barth, though he was usually critical of Barth's developing theology, which in his judgment failed to meet the test of orthodoxy. However, my philosophy teacher and life-long friend, Dr. Henry Stob, shared with me how he had found Barth a powerful rebuttal to the liberalism of Hartford Theological Seminary during his year of postgraduate study. But it was not until I attended the Princeton sessions that I became increasingly aware of the significance of the Barthian revolution in theology that was just making its powerful impact in America. I heard the lectures of Dr. Joseph L. Hromadka from Czechoslovakia, a neo-orthodox theologian, and his striking affirmation that he took every word of the Bible seriously. I was encouraged to learn more about neo-orthodoxy, with its renewed regard for the Scriptures and for the Reformation theology of Luther and Calvin as well as its powerful repudiation of the liberalism and naturalism that dominated so much of the intelligentsia of American Protestantism since the turn of the century. I learned how it was seriously challenging liberalism in the mainline churches and seminaries, resulting in a major revolution in modern Protestant theology. A couple of years later I witnessed the impact of neo-orthodoxy on the campus of Union Theological Seminary in the selection of its speakers, the tenor of its discussions, and the recalcitrance of the few, old liberals still on the campus. Neo-orthodoxy was a far cry from the devastating liberalism of Schweitzer and McConnell.

At the same time I was greatly encouraged to take no radical or hasty action by my reading of Edwin Lewis's *A Christian Manifesto.*[6] Lewis was Professor of Systematic Theology and Philoso-

6. Nashville: Cokesbury, 1934.

phy of Religion at Drew Theological Seminary at Drew University. The book, published a decade before my ordination, was particularly relevant to my needs because the author had once been an advocate of the liberal perspective that eliminated the supernatural and adopted the naturalism that completely rejected Christianity. At some point in mid-career, probably under the impact of neo-orthodoxy, he had come to see liberalism as a needless retreat from historic Christianity and had come to a renewed affirmation of the heritage of the church. His book was a passionate repudiation of his earlier liberalism written with the urgency of a convert. He vigorously exposed the inadequacies of liberalism and reaffirmed the basic Christian faith. Lewis highlighted for me the significance of the resurrection as the impregnable rock on which the Christian faith was validated. That has shaped the direction of my thinking ever since. Lewis's book was for me a source of strength for my belief that it was possible to maintain with intellectual honesty and respectability the heart of the classic, orthodox Christian faith in the modern world.

Dr. Lewis and various other authors were an inspiration to continue believing and ministering as I pursued my defense and understanding of the gospel I had always believed and preached. Throughout the years of my ministry, always with a strong apologetic interest, I attended summer institutes at Princeton Seminary, Union Seminary in New York, McCormick Seminary, and Union Seminary in Virginia that were designed to help pastors keep abreast of current developments in biblical studies and theology. In addition I spent three summers enrolled in classes at Union in New York, where I was privileged to listen to and profit from the mainline luminaries of the time, such as Reinhold Niebuhr, Paul Tillich, John C. Bennett, John Knox, Wilhelm Pauck, Donald Baillie, Hendrik Kraemer, John S. Whale, and others. I was seeking to be true to my commitments to integrity and honesty while drawing on the resources of fellow believers, even if it meant rethinking the formulations of the faith I had been taught.

I found my core beliefs strengthened, though also modified, by the perspectives and insights of these scholarly theologians. I was particularly gratified by and profited greatly from Donald Baillie's *God Was in Christ*[7] and John S. Whale's wonderful little book on *Christian Doctrine*[8] because these books wrestled with issues of modern life but affirmed the basic Christian faith that was at the core of my beliefs. I also profited from the few private conversations that I was privileged to have with these kind and sympathetic teachers. But it was especially J. Gresham Machen's famous *Christianity and Liberalism,*[9] first published in 1923, that encouraged me to believe it was possible to maintain the Christian faith.

In 1959 I spent a semester on sabbatical at New College in Edinburgh attending the classes of Thomas F. Torrance, an eminent theologian and highly recognized Barthian scholar, and the lectures of the famous preacher and New Testament scholar James S. Stewart, who was influenced by and frequently quoted Emil Brunner. Both men enlarged my acquaintance with the primary neo-orthodox theological giants, while also sharing their own strong commitment to and interpretation of the evangelical Christian faith. In lectures and visits, I experienced repeatedly the spiritual benefits of "the communion of the saints."

By contrast, in 1969 I spent a sabbatical semester at the Claremont School of Theology in California — a very liberal school. After twenty-six years in the ministry I wanted to hear about current thought in liberal circles, particularly the challenges of post-Barthian developments in theology. I knew that these developments were issuing in such radical theologies as John A. T. Robinson's *Honest to God*[10] and the short-lived "Death of God" fad in the 1960s. I enrolled in courses with Professor John B. Cobb, who introduced me to the rising eminence of process theology. I audited

7. New York: C. Scribner's Sons, 1948.
8. Cambridge, U.K.: The University Press, 1941.
9. New York: Macmillan, 1923.
10. Philadelphia: Westminster Press, 1963.

a seminar on the Gospel of John with James M. Robinson, a re-
nowned New Testament scholar on the forefront of the new quest
for the historical Jesus and a leading scholar on the *Nag Hammadi*
scrolls discovered in Egypt. I did not profit much from the seminar
except to observe the way liberal New Testament scholarship proceeds with its scientific approach and careful analysis of the biblical text. I appreciated the insights of these scholars, who obviously
disagreed radically with my conservative understanding of the
gospel. Dr. Cobb assured me that while process theology was incompatible with my Reformed heritage, it was not incompatible
with the basic thrust of biblical teaching. Classic Christian theology employed the ontology of Greek philosophy in structuring its
doctrines, he said, while process theology sought to rethink and
restructure the Christian faith in the context of the metaphysics of
Alfred North Whitehead. I found the Whiteheadian concept of
God in many ways more biblically compatible than the abstract,
immovable, absolute God of Greek philosophy that informed orthodox theology.

At Claremont I became aware of the huge chasm between the
teachings of a liberal seminary and the life of the church. Dr. Cobb
once spoke in class about the plight of graduates who imbibed the
liberal perspectives of the seminary and would enter the church as
pastors. They would find their learning so far from the life and
faith of the congregation that they would soon leave the ministry
or quickly forget their seminary education and lapse into the resi-
due of whatever conservative Christian theology was still present
in the church — and, I may add, they would probably endure a
hypocritical dichotomy that would eviscerate their ministry. It
was not an enviable time for graduates of liberal seminaries. It
spoke to me about the irrelevance of liberal Christianity and how
dispirited many of the mainline churches and their pastors had
become in the radical 1960s and 1970s.

I am deeply grateful for the opportunities I had to hear so
many leading and diverse theologians and biblical scholars as I

16

continued to wrestle with my commitment to the Christian faith in the contemporary, secularized world. I have learned much from the perspectives and commitments of these men who possessed far greater learning than I. I was also helped by my wide reading of continental and British as well as North American theologians. Lest I appear more learned than I am, let me hasten to confess that my reading was often selective and superficial, looking for data bearing on the state of my current thought or my immediate sermonic needs. It had to be done while serving a large and busy church, preaching twice most Sundays, visiting the sick and counseling the needy, engaging in denominational assignments (which I considered my recreation), as well as fulfilling my role in my family, which was unfortunately too often shortchanged.

Among the benefits of these encounters and my reading was to learn that most, though not all, of these learned scholars had begun their theological pilgrimage from the same conservative, orthodox base as my own. Even the most liberal among them had struggled with the tension between the Christian faith and the modern world that fueled my search for understanding. They differed dramatically in their attempts to harmonize the Christian faith with the learning of the modern world. Some scholars arrived at positions that I deemed attractive, and others virtually jettisoned the gospel to accommodate to the spirit of modernity. Yet I recognized that even those in the latter category meant to be Christian, seeking to salvage something of the gospel they believed compatible with modern learning. There have been theologians who felt compelled to surrender the Christian faith completely and consequentially pursued other careers, such as Joseph Fletcher of *Situation Ethics* fame and William Hamilton, a "Death of God" theologian. I sensed there were more liberal ministers and dispirited professors who would leave their positions having surrendered their beliefs but for the necessities of livelihood and family commitments.

What impressed me was that many of these scholars were not out to reject and destroy the Christian faith, but instead to defend it as the truth in some form compatible with the modern world. They felt they had to accommodate and make concessions to the modern mind if honesty and integrity required it, while at the same time they meant to be committed to some form of revelation in Jesus Christ. No doubt there were and are those who at the price of rejecting their Christian moorings have become bitter, angry, and even hateful of Christianity and the church. Schweitzer had pointed this out long ago.

One summer some years ago, I attended an Institute at Union Theological Seminary in Richmond, Virginia, where a professor from Harvard Divinity School lectured. In one of our afternoon sessions with the lecturer, I related how a prominent, liberal critic in Grand Rapids who openly denied the Christian faith criticized many so-called liberal theologians and pastors for their halfway attempts to accommodate both the Christian faith and the modern world. This critic was convinced that once a person leaves the utterly absurd stance of an infallible Bible and its literal reading, in honesty she must go all the way down the slippery slope to Naturalism. There is no respectable halfway house that allows for a mediating stance, the critic was certain. I then turned to the professor and opined that he had been reared in a conservative Lutheran family and now held a mediating position in theology. He affirmed quickly the devout and conservative orthodoxy of his parents. "What," I asked, "keeps you from going the whole way down the slippery slope?" The group appeared to acknowledge I had raised a fundamental and intensely personal question, but the hour was ended. The following morning at breakfast, the professor sought a seat next to me and said, "Yesterday you asked me the question of my life." I knew I was talking to a fellow believer who was struggling with the same fundamental questions that had so often gnawed at my mind. I was reminded that my crisis of faith is the crisis confronting so many thoughtful Christians in the modern world. What, I asked, keeps so many mediating theologians from going the whole way? Is there after all an underlying reasonableness in Christianity that is not easily dismissed? Does it address and fulfill a deeply felt need of the human heart and mind? Does the modern scientific world leave too many loose ends in its perspectives on human life? Are there fundamental realities of existence that cannot be denied but are not addressed by the perspectives of the modern world?

In the kaleidoscopic world of twentieth-century theology I kept wondering what my confession would be at the end of my ministry. It was the recollection of this question that surfaced when in my farewell comments I testified to my colleagues that I still believed the gospel. Having reached retirement age I could confess I continued to maintain the fundamental truths of the Christian faith as revealed in the Holy Scriptures and confessed by the church through the centuries. These revealed truths constituted the core of the beliefs and the faith I had preached and taught, the ground of the hope I shared in my pastoral work, and the inspiration that encouraged me through the years to love and serve the diverse membership and varied needs of my congregation. Even now this writing in my old age may be another attempt to reexamine, clarify, and think through my defense of Christianity and reason for believing the gospel — my personal apologetics — that I have developed through the years. It is this defense that continues to underlie, affirm, and bolster my commitment to the Christian faith.

It is not that I have satisfactory answers to all my doubts. Nor have I adequately answered all the powerful assaults on the Christian faith in the twentieth century. Throughout my entire ministry I have struggled to defend and articulate a defense of the Christian faith that I believed was reasonable and could be maintained with integrity. But I must also confess that with multitudes of believers through the ages, I have frequently echoed the prayer of the tormented father of the epileptic child who cried, "(Lord), I believe, help my unbelief!" (Mark 9:24). I had to learn that faith always has room for questions, doubts, and uncertainties or it is no longer faith, just as doubt contains an element of faith or it is no longer doubt.

With the expansion of our knowledge, the areas of faith and doubt are reduced. There was a time when people believed either that the earth is flat or that it is round. Science has established the earth is round; it is no longer a question of belief. Science has been less successful in diminishing faith and doubt in the studies of history, social studies, psychology, and religion because these defy the methods of scientific exploration to achieve the certitude of knowledge. In these areas of our existence we propose working hypotheses to explain tentatively certain facts, and we base our assumptions for action or conduct upon them.

In 1930, when I was thirteen, I read that Pluto was discovered by a young astronomer, barely out of his teen years, Clyde W. Tombaugh. Already in 1919 an earlier astronomer had predicted its probable existence from the perturbations in the orbits of Neptune and Uranus. These orbital irregularities caused by some force did not prove the existence of Pluto but were evidences that made its existence highly probable. After the discovery of Pluto the orbital perturbations were known to be the result of Pluto's existence. The example of Pluto's discovery I found analogous to positing the existence of God from our experience of all the evidences that we cannot account for within the natural order. Like Pluto before its discovery, God remains an unproven hypothesis of a reasonable faith.

It is important to understand that it is not possible to prove the truth of the Christian faith any more than we can prove the truths of interpersonal relationships. The relations between persons are based on faith and trust, not reasoned proof. Of course, in a good relationship such faith and trust are usually supported by reasonable evidence.

Marriage is an example of a faith commitment based on reasonable grounds established by facts and experience. Prior to accepting a proposal of marriage, a woman has supposedly ascertained enough facts about her suitor and experienced sufficient evidence of his behavior, trustworthiness, and affection to accept his hand in marriage. At the same time she is aware that he is a free agent and her marriage to him rests on faith, trust, and love. In a good marriage the experience of faith and love in time achieves for all practical purposes the equivalence of proof. So it was in the instance of the Apostle Paul's faith in Jesus Christ when he testified: "I know the one in whom I have put my trust, and am sure that he is able to guard until that day what I have entrusted to him" (2 Timothy 1:12). For many Christians, trust in the gospel reaches a stage where they have such strong conviction that unbelief is inconceivable.

I have always been eager to affirm that Christianity is not unreasonable to believe while living in the modern world. It has been a lifelong concern of mine to be true to the first letter of Peter where we are urged, "Always be ready to make your defense to anyone who demands from you an account of the hope that is in you" (3:15). Already in college I learned from my teacher and mentor, my lifelong best friend and colleague, Dr. Henry Stob, that our best defense of the Christian faith is to invite others to stand with us on our pinnacle of faith and survey the totality of our existence from the Christian perspective. From that vantage point we can see that the panorama of life and reality is more satisfying and fulfilling of our basic needs for meaning and purpose than any other worldview.

I confess I have not remained unchanged in my allegiance to the precise formulations of Christian doctrines as I was taught them and understood them when I began my ministry. Sixty years of wide reading and biblical study, critical and probing reflection, hearing lectures and attending seminars, engaging in discussions with other believers and avowed unbelievers, and meeting and conversing with adherents of other religions have made me question and rethink my understanding of the Christian faith. But after years of study and reflection, pastoral and personal experiences, I have also been strengthened in my basic Christian commitment. Not least, let me acknowledge, it was often through the intimacy of close and trusted friendships in which we shared doubts and convictions, aired critical questions, and proposed answers that I profited greatly from the insights, affirmations, and convictions of others. I have been greatly blessed with intelligent and learned Christian friends, with whom I could discuss my questions and debate issues of mutual concern. With the Apostles' Creed I gladly confess the efficacy of "the communion of saints."

I remain committed to the basic truth of the gospel as revealed in the Scriptures and incorporated in the historic creeds, condensed in the Apostles' Creed, the truth that may be summed up in the powerful affirmation of the Apostle Paul: "God was in Christ reconciling the world unto himself" (2 Corinthians 5:19). My lifelong experience is compatible, I believe, with Christian living as the Scriptures teach: "You therefore, beloved, since you are forewarned, beware that you are not carried away with the error of the lawless and lose your own stability. *But grow in the grace and knowledge of our Lord and Savior Jesus Christ*" (2 Peter 3:17, 18).

Were I to describe my theological position today I would identify with what might be called "modern orthodoxy" or "liberal evangelicalism." William Hordern in 1960 wrote of a growing number of theologians that were seeking a way between fundamentalism, liberalism and neo-orthodoxy who accepted orthodoxy as a growing tradition. He refers to this movement as "modern orthodoxy." Hordern writes:

> . . . it must not be thought that the position is derived at by first weighing the modern movements in theology and taking the best out of each. The heart of the movement lies in

loyalty to the faith of historic orthodoxy, not because it is ancient orthodoxy, but because it is believed to be true. Modern Orthodoxy believes that in the orthodox tradition we have a precious heritage of truth which must not be overthrown just because someone has split the atom and someone else has looked farther through a telescope. Nevertheless, it is willing to understand the old truth more fully in so far as modern thought makes that possible.[11]

I take as my own the testimony of the distinguished theologian/scientist, Thomas F. Torrance, when he writes in his *Space, Time and Resurrection:*

I make no apology for taking divine revelation seriously. If God really is God, the Creator of all things visible and invisible and the Source of all rational order in the universe, I find it absurd to think that he does not actively reveal himself to us but remains inert and aloof, so that we are left to grope about in the dark for possible intimations and clues to his reality which we may use in trying to establish arguments for his existence. I do not deny that there is a proper place for rational argumentation in what is traditionally known as 'natural theology,' for I find it contradictory to operate with a deistic disjunction between God and the universe, which presupposes belief in the existence of God but assumes at the same time that he is utterly detached and unknowable. . . . I find it absurd to think that God does not freely act within the framework of space and time, or the intelligible structures of what he had created, in making himself known to mankind. If God really is God, the living Creator of us all, not only is he intelligibly accessible to our understanding

11. *A Layman's Guide to Protestant Theology* (New York: Macmillan, 1956), pp. 185-86.

but actively at work within the world revealing himself to those to whom he has made for communion with himself. Divine revelation and intelligible content belong inseparably together.[12]

12. Grand Rapids: Eerdmans, 1976, pp. 1-2.

The Resurrection of Jesus:
The Pivot of Faith

━━━╾⟨ᴑᴑᴑ⟩╼━━━

I do not remember when, but at some point I was impressed that both Schweitzer and McConnell had little if anything to say about the resurrection of Jesus. At the same time I found the New Testament saturated with it and with the "livingness" of Christ that is foundational to and indispensable for the Christian faith from the New Testament perspective. The origins of the Christian church arose out of the conviction that the crucified Jesus was resurrected from the dead. So I asked what Schweitzer and McConnell did with the Easter accounts present in all four Gospels and explicitly taught by the Apostle Paul: "And if Christ has not been raised, then our proclamation has been in vain and your faith has been in vain. We are even found to be misrepresenting God, because we testified of God that he raised Christ — whom he did not raise if it is true that the dead are not raised. For if the dead are not raised, then Christ has not been raised. If Christ has not been raised, then faith is futile and you are still in your sins" (1 Corinthians 15:14-17). I observed that neither one addressed the biblical testimony of the resurrection nor sought to solve the vexing riddle of how the Jesus of history became the Christ of faith apart from his bodily resurrection. Why? What explains their rejection of the resurrection?

McConnell clearly states that it was his *Zeitgeist* that ruled out for him the possibility of miracles, including the resurrection. The same was undoubtedly true for Schweitzer. Apparently so firmly established in their minds was the modern *a priori* denial of the supernatural that both Schweitzer and McConnell deemed it unnecessary to refute what seemed to them to be the patent absurdity of a bodily resurrection. However moving and inspirational are the words of Schweitzer, they do not hide the fact that he did not believe God raised Jesus from the dead as the New Testament teaches. For him Jesus lives on in the spirit of his life and words — just like the Buddha, Confucius, and Muhammad. But the words of Buddha, Confucius, and Muhammad live on by the appeal of their worldviews and prescribed patterns for living. Why does the spirit of Jesus live on when his life and teaching were so geared to his "lunacy" of Messiahship and the coming of God's kingdom in and through himself, as Schweitzer interpreted it? The fact is that Jesus' life and teachings gained relevance in the early church only after his death and reported resurrection. Without belief in the resurrection, in all probability his life and teachings would never have survived beyond his generation. Thus the crucial question is: Apart from the resurrection, would Christianity have become the world's foremost religion? Is not the resurrection at the heart of Christianity? Is it not indispensable for the living of our lives with meaning, purpose, and hope? I am convinced it would be hard to overestimate the importance for the church and human existence whether we affirm or deny the resurrection of Jesus Christ.

Christianity, in distinction from all other religions, is not first of all commitment to a body of truths — although it is certainly that. All other religions are based on the teachings of some spiritual genius or inspired teacher who, claiming divine revelation, presented a worldview that seeks to account for human life in the universe and teaches a consequent pattern for living. To be a Christian, however, is to be in union with the living person of Jesus Christ. It is confessed beautifully in the first question and answer of the irenic Heidelberg Catechism: "What is your only comfort in life and in death? That I belong — body and soul, in life and in death — not to myself, but to my faithful Savior, Jesus Christ. . . . Because I belong to him, Christ, by his Holy Spirit . . . makes me whole-heartedly willing and ready from now on to live for him." In the preface to his book *Union with Christ*,[1] Lewis Smedes writes:

> How can a person who lived nearly two thousand years ago radically change a human life here and now? . . . Does the Jesus of the past become, in fact, the Jesus of the present? The Apostle Paul says that He does. And this is the difference between His influence and that of any other influential person. He touches us here and now, not merely by the ripples of the historical currents He once set in motion, but by entering into union with us personally. Union with Christ — this is the sum and substance of the Christian's status, the definition of his relationship to Jesus, the large reality in which all the nuances of his new being are embraced. (p. xi)

Such is the testimony of the Christian church through the ages grounded on the gospel of Jesus' resurrection. The questions and mysteries that faith in the living person of Christ raises we may consider later. First we must consider the centrality of the resurrection as the *sine qua non* for Christian faith and life and the supreme moment of God's revelation of himself for union with us.

Some years back I attended as an observer a regional Faith and Order seminar north of Chicago, Illinois, sponsored by the World Council of Churches on the Lima Statement of 1982 on Baptism, Eucharist, and Ministry. Prior to the plenary sessions we were divided into small groups to study and reflect on the agenda and to report at the plenary. My group included two Roman Catholic priests, several Protestant theologians, and clergy of diverse main-

---

1. Grand Rapids: Eerdmans, 1970.

line denominations. Having come to the end of our assignment early with a little time left, I raised the question: What is it that brings us together, and what do we have in common that unites us in such a study group? One of the priests immediately responded, "Jesus Christ." All acknowledged that he was our common bond. I asked further if we all could find unity in Paul's confession that "God was in Christ reconciling the world unto himself." On this too we all agreed. The Methodist theologian added that he preferred Paul's statement to merely saying "Jesus Christ" because it opened the doors of salvation wider than the name itself implies.

The session was then at an end so we pursued the issue no further, but upon reflection it occurred to me that as soon as we would have sought to expand on any aspect of Paul's affirmation, our theological differences and denominational divisions concerning Christ and his role in the church and society would have become evident. But what impressed me was that even though Jesus lived two millennia ago, and our interpretation and understanding of him had fragmented us into innumerable denominations, he is still the dynamic center and inspiring, cohesive personal basis of the entire Christian community to this day! That encounter reinforced my conviction that at the heart of the gospel, the core of Christian belief, the center of the church's life, its missionary challenge, is a person who lived in history: Jesus Christ, who still lives as Savior and Lord. In the words of Carl E. Braaten, "The flaming center of the Christian message is Jesus, the Christ of God, the Savior of mankind and the Lord of history. Our overriding concern is to remind the church of its task to proclaim this message to all nations until the end of history."[2] This affirmation is all-important particularly in the current climate of a renewed liberal ferment that denies the uniqueness of Christ and the absoluteness of Christianity. Such a trajectory begins with denying the uniqueness of the resurrection.

2. *The Flaming Center* (Philadelphia: Fortress, 1977), p. 2.

The Resurrection of Jesus: The Pivot of Faith

In distinction from all religions based on the teachings and perspectives of long-dead founders, it is essential to understand that the heart of the Christian faith is not first of all commitment to creeds but to the living person of Jesus Christ as our risen Lord, to whom the creeds bear witness, and through whose affirmations we are introduced to the living Lord. As a pastor during World War II I visited the wife of a serviceman, whose husband was away for four long years. While in the service his daughter was born; she knew him only as a picture. Asked where daddy was, she would point to his picture. At the time he was not a living person in her life. It was later as she grew older and after he returned from the service that she came to identify him as her living father. To be a Christian is to know Jesus Christ the living Lord of our lives, whom we worship along with God the Father; to whom we pray and in whose name we pray; by whose power we seek to live our lives. As the little girl had to make the transition from her father as a picture to her father as a living person, so Christians need to make the transition from the Jesus of the Scriptures and the creeds to the living Lord and Savior of their lives.

The resurrection of Jesus is the key consideration in any discussion of the Christian faith. It is the resurrection that explains how the Jesus of history has become the Christ of our faith, the Savior and Lord of our lives. It was this truth on which my commitment pivoted as I continued my studies — a point re-enforced by numerous theologians and New Testament scholars. Hans Küng addresses this uniqueness of Jesus Christ:

> Why did there arise that bond to the Master which is so very different from the bonds of other movements to the personalities of their founders, as for instance of Marxists to Marx, or enthusiastic Freudians to Freud? Why is Jesus not merely venerated, studied and followed as the founder and teacher who lived years ago, but — especially in the worshiping congregation — proclaimed as alive and known as the one who

is active at the present time? How did the extraordinary idea arise that he himself leads his followers, his community, through his Spirit?

In a word then, we are faced with the historical enigma of the emergence, the beginning, the origin, of Christianity. How different this was from the gradual, peaceful propagation of the teachings of the successful sages, Buddha and Confucius; how different from the largely violent propagation of the teachings of the victorious Muhammad. And all this within the lifetime of the founders. How different, after a complete failure and a shameful death, were the spontaneous emergence and almost explosive propagation of this message and community in the very name of the defeated leader. After the disastrous outcome of this life, what gave the initial impetus to that unique world-historical development: a truly world-transforming religion emerging from the gallows where a man was hanged in shame? . . . it becomes clear that this *Passion story* with its disastrous outcome — why should it have entered into the memory of mankind? — was transmitted only because there was also an *Easter story* which made the Passion story (and the story of the action lying behind it) appear in a completely different light. [3]

Jürgen Moltmann writes in his famous *Theology of Hope*,[4]

Christianity stands or falls with the reality of the raising of Jesus from the dead by God. In the New Testament there is no faith that does not start *a priori* with the resurrection of Jesus. Paul is clearly taking over a basic form of the primitive Christian confession when he says in Rom. 10:9: "If thou

---

3. *On Being a Christian* (Garden City, N.Y.: Doubleday, 1976), p. 345.
4. New York: Harper and Row, 1967, pp. 165-66.

shalt confess with thy mouth the Lord Jesus, and shall believe in thine heart that God hath raised him from the dead, thou shalt be saved." The confession to the person of Jesus as the Lord and the confession to the work of God who raised him from the dead belong inseparably together, although the two formulae do not coincide but mutually expound each other. A Christian faith that is not resurrection faith can therefore be called neither Christian nor faith. It is the knowledge of the risen Christ and the confession of him who raised him that form the basis on which the memory of the life, work, sufferings and death of Jesus is kept alive and presented in the gospels. It is the recognition of the risen Christ that gives rise to the Church's recognition of its own commission in the mission to the nations. It is the remembrance of his resurrection that is the ground of the inclusive hope in the universal future of Christ.

James D. Smart, Professor Emeritus of Biblical Interpretation at Union Theological Seminary, New York, likewise confirms in his *The Recovery of Humanity* the unique significance of the resurrected Christ for Christianity:

There is no point at which present-day Christianity stands in sharper contrast to New Testament Christianity than in the place it gives to the resurrection. In the New Testament Church the resurrection was at the center. It determined the day of worship. The first Christians worshiped on Sunday instead of on the Jewish Sabbath, Saturday, because on the first day of the week Jesus arose from the dead. Their faith in Jesus as the Messiah rested primarily, not upon anything in the story of his life, but upon the manifestation of his divine power in the resurrection. The crucifixion left the disciples puzzled and disillusioned, but with the resurrection they knew once and for all who it was that had been in their midst. So also for Paul, it was the appearance to him of the risen and living Lord that changed him from the chief persecutor of the faith into its chief apostle. In the New Testament everything hinges on the resurrection. The gospel that is preached is not a reproduction of Jesus' teachings or of his original announcement of the Kingdom, although it included both of these, but primarily it is the proclamation of the Lordship of Jesus Christ, revealed as Lord by his resurrection from the dead, and the new world into which men enter by faith when they accept him as their Lord. Take away the resurrection of Jesus from the New Testament and you do not merely drop out one among many elements of the story; rather, it is as though you took away the hub into which all the spokes of the wheel are fitted.[5]

Prior to the eighteenth century the church, whether Roman Catholic, Orthodox, or Protestant, centered in the worship, teaching, and mission of Jesus Christ, the living resurrected Savior and Lord, as known from the proclamation of the gospel, taught in the New Testament, and remembered in the holy sacraments. The Christian faith as a living religious response was not directed to the historical facts of Jesus' short career of teaching and healing but to his death and resurrection, as is evident in the Apostles' Creed, which moves directly from his virgin birth to his sufferings and death and resurrection, with no reference to his teaching and healing ministry. The heart of the gospel was that Almighty God, the Creator, was in the Jesus of history reconciling the fallen world unto himself through his crucifixion, death, and resurrection, whereby he became the Christ of faith as Savior and Lord of all who believed the gospel. The church in its proclamation of the Christ of faith and in its remembrance of him through the sacraments was understood

5. Philadelphia: Westminster Press, 1953, pp. 151-52.

to be Christ's body on earth to bring God's salvation and lordship to fruition in the lives of believers. Salvation came through the resurrected Christ.

All of which, of course, is not to say that the life of Jesus is of no great significance in the church. The life of Jesus as presented in the Gospels is first of all tremendously important in providing the setting for his death and resurrection and their significance in the divine economy of the world's redemption. But in addition the life of Jesus Christ serves the church and believers with a pattern for and example of godly living. He is our example in his trust in and love for the Heavenly Father, in his obedience and service in the kingdom of God, and in his commitment to and sacrifice for others. As believers we are called to be imitators of Christ the Lord (1 Thessalonians 1:6).

Fundamental to faith in the resurrection is belief in a personal God, who as Creator and Sustainer of our universe is sovereign and free to raise Jesus from the dead. To bolster this belief religious philosophers and theologians have throughout the history of the church advanced rational arguments for God's existence. They are primarily the well-known ontological, cosmological, and teleological arguments. It is generally agreed, although by no means universally, that since the critiques of David Hume and Immanuel Kant these arguments are flawed as proofs for God's existence. Agnostics and atheists are quick to point out their invalidity. Kant, of course, also advanced the moral argument as evidence for God's existence, which C. S. Lewis used with great effectiveness in *The Case for Christianity*.[6]

Alasdair MacIntyre agrees that a fallacious argument points nowhere and three fallacious arguments are no better than one. He explains that "the proofs . . . attempt to state in formal terms and render intellectually cogent certain facets of the religious frame of mind . . . [in which the believer's] vision of the universe

---

6. New York: Macmillan, 1948.

engages his imagination so powerfully that he cannot envisage the non-existence of God as a genuine possibility."[7]

But apart from the logical fallacies that may invalidate them, there is the additional problem that what these classical arguments purport to prove is not the God of the Christian faith, the personal God of love and justice who has revealed himself to humanity in Jesus Christ. Believers generally have viewed these arguments as strong testimonies, persuasive evidences or pointers, supporting belief in God's existence as a reasonable supposition and thereby undermining the case for atheism, even though atheists generally remain unimpressed by these arguments. Despite the arrogance of atheists who are overly impressed with their intellectual superiority and integrity, the issue of God's existence does not depend on one's intellectual capacity or learning. It was reported some time ago that Carl Sagan, well-known astronomer and vocally avowed atheist, once said to Joan Brown Campbell, then general secretary of the National Council of Christian Churches, that he could not understand how such an intelligent woman could believe in God. To which Ms. Campbell replied that she could not understand how anyone as intelligent as Carl Sagan *did not* believe in God. More than intelligence is involved in the faith of our choice.

But what about the resurrection as an argument for God's existence? How compelling is it as a factor *in history* that provides powerful evidence for the reality of a supernatural, personal God to account for its occurrence? The thesis of this monograph is that the resurrection of Jesus is a strong, if not the strongest, apologetic for the truth of the Christian faith, and for the finality of Christianity among the religions of the world. The resurrection — if true — is, in my judgment, not only a most convincing argument for the existence of God, but even more, reveals to us the nature, character, and purposes of God through the revelation of himself in Jesus Christ. Jesus said, "Whoever has seen me has seen

---

7. *Difficulties in Christian Belief* (London: SCM Press, 1959), p. 63.

the Father" (John 14:9). The light of the supernatural world of God disclosed in the resurrection of Jesus illumines human existence more effectively than any other worldview.

While I have long felt the truth of this thesis, the resurrection is not, to the best of my knowledge, often advanced or defended from this perspective. For example, Charles C. Anderson reports in his *The Historical Jesus: A Continuing Quest*[8] concerning the position of George E. Ladd, a conservative theologian, who advanced a typical approach to the truth of the resurrection of Jesus:

> As Ladd has noticed, it all boils down to the way in which one looks at God in his relation to the world. If God is deistically removed from our world, then it would be impossible for him to intervene in its workings. If this be the case, the resurrection must be rejected in the same way as miracles and all special revelation. If, on the other hand, God is identified with our world in a pantheistic sort of way, he loses any existence separate from it, and any "interference" with it is automatically ruled out. If, however, God is at once actively involved in our world, and yet, maintains an existence separate from it, the possibility of the resurrection as well as that of miracles may be retained.

In other words, Ladd is saying that belief in the resurrection depends upon your prior view of God and the world. But it is my thesis that in the resurrection of Jesus the existence of God and his relationship to the world are evidenced in history and in Christian experience more clearly and decisively than by any other argumentation.

Daniel Jenkins, in *Believing in God,* insists that

> . . . it must be realized that the evidence provided by Jesus is of the first importance in answering the question of God's

8. Grand Rapids: Eerdmans, 1972, pp. 156-57.

reality. It is sometimes assumed that what we make of the impact of Jesus depends on the attitude toward God's existence that we bring to it, an attitude reached on other grounds. The truth is that the impact of Jesus itself provides essential evidence in helping us decide whether we believe in God.

It is essential that we see how the whole question concerning the reality of the Christian God gathers to a head in the cross and resurrection of Christ. . . . Nowhere is the reality of God and the covenant he made with Israel put to the test more searchingly than in these tremendous events. All the threats to meaning in human life are gathered up in the expiring cry of Jesus as he hangs upon the cross, "My God, my God, why hast thou forsaken me?" And all the hopes of the fulfillment of true life in eternity go with his lifeless body into the tomb. If Jesus lived and died in vain, the Christian God does not exist.

It was out of the conviction that God in Jesus Christ has proved himself stronger than the cross and the tomb, that the Christian faith was born. The evidence for this conviction is given in the resurrection experience, which was the supreme vindication of the faith of Jesus. This is why Easter has always been recognized as the most distinctive festival of the Church's life and *why, in its periods of clear vision, the Church has always insisted that belief in the Christian God depends on the knowledge of the risen Christ.*[9] (Italics added)

This argumentation is in keeping with Jesus' testimony in John 12:44-46: "Then Jesus cried out, 'When a man believes in me, he does not believe in me only, but in the one who sent me. When he looks at me, he sees the one who sent me. I have come into the world as a light, so that no one who believes in me should stay in darkness.'"

9. Philadelphia: Westminster Press, 1956, pp. 44-46.

The Resurrection of Jesus: The Pivot of Faith

It is instructive that the resurrection anchored Karl Barth in his theology when he broke with the liberalism of his day in the early twentieth century and revolutionized the theological world. Karl Barth was reared and educated in the Germany that produced the theological fruits of the Enlightenment in such giants as Schleiermacher, Strauss, Ritschl, Harnack, Schweitzer, and Troeltsch. Barth knew how the acids of modernity had eaten the core out of the Christianity of the ages — and as a student he accepted it. It was World War I that precipitated a crisis for the young preacher. Struck with the failure of liberalism in that devastating time, he turned to a renewed study of the Scriptures and the theologians of the Reformation. Holmes Rolston in his early book on Karl Barth pointed out that one of the organizing principles of Barthian thought was

> the existence of another world, the world of God that stands in utter contradiction to the world of man. He is sure that we must start from the belief in the existence of this world of God and that only as we start with this assumption are we able to come to an understanding of the world of man. . . . The closest thing that we have to a positive disclosure of the nature of the life of the world of eternity is found in the resurrection life of Christ. . . . In the risen Christ a form of life touched this world which was quite different from anything that the world had ever seen. . . . The Barthian thought is that in the resurrection of Christ we have a revelation of the world of eternity in the world of time. . . . The Barthian thought in its essence flows from the recognition of this difference. . . . The assumption that such a world as that revealed in the resurrection life of Christ does exist is basic to the Christian faith.[10]

10. *A Conservative Looks to Barth and Brunner* (Nashville: Cokesbury, 1933), pp. 31-36.

Thomas F. Torrance, in his preface to *Space, Time and Resurrection*,[11] tells of his last visit with Karl Barth prior to his death, in which Barth reaffirmed his belief in the bodily resurrection of Jesus as pivotal to his theology:

> We went on to talk about . . . [how] "the scientific starting point" in theology that . . . he had adopted was *the resurrection of Christ*. The reason for that answer Barth had often given: it was from the perspective of the resurrection that the whole of the New Testament presentation of Christ is shaped, and it is still from the event of the resurrection that Jesus Christ and his being and action in life and death penetrate to us, "thus becoming truth in their reality, and as truth reality for the world" (*Church Dogmatics,* IV/3, p. 284). Then I ventured to say that unless that starting point was closely bound up with *the incarnation,* it might be only too easy, judging from many of our contemporaries and even some of his former students, to think of the resurrection after all in a rather docetic way, lacking concrete ontological reality. But at that remark, Barth leaned over to me and said with considerable force, which I shall never forget, *'Wohlverstanden, leibliche Auferstehung'* — "Mark well, bodily resurrection." Karl Barth died at prayer in that room a few weeks later. (pp. x, xi)

Lewis Smedes, in his last book, *My God and I,*[12] tells of his visit with Karl Barth and writes concerning Barth's conviction about the reality of the bodily resurrection of Jesus:

> I had occasion to put the question to Barth himself: "Sir, if you will permit me an absurd anachronism, let us suppose

11. Grand Rapids: Eerdmans, 1976.
12. Grand Rapids: Eerdmans, 2003.

that a journalist carried a camera into Jesus' tomb about eight o'clock on Easter Sunday morning and took pictures of every inch of the tomb, what would have showed up on his film?" Barth sighed. This again? He had been asked questions like this by every skeptical evangelical who got within shouting distance of him. But he was patient: "He would have gotten nothing but pictures of an empty tomb. Jesus was not there. He had walked out of the tomb early that morning." (p. 69)

It would be difficult to overestimate, if true, the significance of the resurrection for our understanding of human existence. Some years ago an article appeared in *The Atlantic Monthly* entitled: "What Makes News?" in which its author, T. S. Matthew, wrote:

> The only big news, private or public, that human beings are really concerned about is news of life and death. . . . There has been no news on either subject for some time — nearly two thousand years, in fact. The Resurrection was tremendous good news, if true, the best ever reported.

If true? This is the crucial question for historic, confessional Christianity, the existence and life of the church, and the Christian's vision and understanding of God, the world, its history, and human life, as well as for the living of our days and hope in our dying. In fact, if true, it is the greatest news of all time, to be shared with all people.

Our existence is a bewildering mystery. Who are we? Where did we come from? Why are we here? Where are we going? How shall we live? It is no wonder that the resurrection, if true, is the greatest news ever, because it illumines all of these profound mysteries of our existence. It opens a window to the light of the supernatural, transcendent world of the creating, redeeming God by whose light is revealed our meaning and purpose, our salvation

39

and destiny as citizens of this transitory world. For twenty centuries it has been the faith and hope of Christians, providing direction and comfort to their lives and in the face of death hope in the eternal love of God.

But is it true? Is it reasonable to believe in the bodily resurrection of Jesus? Dead people never become alive; the ancients knew that as well as the modern scientist. In the entire and long history of the world no one has ever died and come back, except as alleged in some ancient myths and a few reported instances of resuscitation in Scripture. In recent times, with the advances in medical science, the clinically dead in rare instances have been revived within a few minutes of death, if only to live a little longer. But the reported resurrection of Jesus was not a resuscitation but a return to life in a new form of existence in continuity with his earthly existence but mysteriously elevated beyond the confines of this world as depicted in the Scriptures. It was more like the metamorphosis of a larva into a butterfly in the insect world. Indeed, if true, the resurrection is the greatest news ever because it illumines the mystery of our living and casts light on the anguish of our dying — the perplexing and disquieting root mysteries of human existence. Did the resurrection really happen as Christians have believed, or was it somehow a projection of wishful thinking in a superstitious age that is unbelievable for people in the modern era? *Is it reasonable, and is there substantial evidence, to believe in the one such event of unique singularity in the long history of the world?*

As late as 1958, after nearly two millennia, Huston Smith could still say, "Most Christians today continue to believe in the bodily resurrection of Christ."[13] The resurrection of Jesus remains an enormously important and indispensable factor in the historical interpretation and understanding of today's world two thousand years later, as well as in the continuing vitality and viability of the

13. *The Religions of Man* (New York: Harper, 1958), p. 312.

church. James S. Stewart asserts the decisive significance of the resurrection and sees it in cosmic perspective in *A Faith to Proclaim:*

> Never did the apostles make the mistake, all too common today, of regarding the Resurrection as a mere epilogue to the Gospel, an addendum to the scheme of salvation, a providential afterthought of God, a codicil to the divine last will and testament. This is to falsify disastrously the whole emphasis of the Bible. Not as an appendix to the faith was the Resurrection ever preached in the apostolic Church. The one and only God the apostles worshipped was the God of the Resurrection. The one and only Gospel they were commissioned to preach was the overpowering, magnificent good news of the Resurrection. . . . When Christ left the grave, it was not merely an announcement that there is a hereafter and a life beyond — which in any case they knew already; it was the shattering of history by a creative act of God Almighty. In this cosmic event, as Paul saw and proclaimed, God was doing something comparable only with what He had done at the first creation. This was the beginning of a new era for the universe, the decisive turning-point for the human race.[14]

---

14. New York: Charles Scribner's Sons, 1953, pp. 105-6.

☧ III ☧

Modern Denial of
the Resurrection of Jesus

—⟨⟨∾∾⟩⟩—

E ver since the resurrection of Jesus was reported, its truth has
been questioned. Its denial is not a modern phenomenon,
and understandably so. Everyone knows that dead people never
become alive again — no exceptions. The Gospels themselves record the doubts and unbelief that arose among the disciples
when the resurrection was first announced. Through the centuries critics have rejected belief in the bodily resurrection of Jesus
with numerous oft-repeated arguments that have challenged believers and reassured unbelievers in their unbelief. I had to take
note of these criticisms in my quest for a reasonable Christian
faith.

Today the larger and more challenging opposition to the resurrection that believers face is the modern scientific, philosophical, and theological objections to belief that are the mainspring of
its widespread disbelief. This is especially true for what Mark Noll
called a philosophical naturalism that masquerades as empirical
science and aggressively denies all supernaturalism. Whatever
belief in God that may be still tolerated is deistic: the belief that
God exists as the Creator of the world but does not interfere with
its operation nor assume any role in the lives of people. Deism rejects all divine revelation and authority, and for practical pur-

poses is atheistic. The familiar analogy is that of the watchmaker, who once having made the watch with its built-in, wound-up spring has nothing further to do with it. The popular modern denial of the resurrection is rooted in this secular worldview that has captivated the modern mind. On its accepted premises the resurrection could not happen, and therefore obviously did not happen. Rudolf Bultmann, often considered the leading New Testament scholar of the twentieth century, viewed the bodily resurrection of Jesus as a mythical event that is as incredible as the resuscitation of a corpse.

Following the revival of art, literature, and learning in Europe known as the Renaissance in the thirteenth through sixteenth centuries came the Enlightenment, or Age of Reason, in the seventeenth and eighteenth centuries, characterized by rationalism and empiricism. With the advances of science that shaped the modern mind, there was engendered a spirit of skepticism that declared axiomatically false anything contrary to logical reasoning and not subject to the scientific methods of verification. Therefore being committed to anti-supernaturalism, the modern mind denied the validity of divine revelation as a source of knowledge and rejected the possibility of divine intervention in human lives and world affairs. Consequently, the actuality of the resurrection as a divine miracle was denied. Based simply on its own premises, the modern mind dogmatically prejudged the resurrection to be impossible, and therefore held that it could not and did not happen!

Modern learning shaped by the *Zeitgeist* of the Enlightenment, having rejected the possibility of miracles, judged belief in a transcendent, supernatural world as primitive superstition. From its standpoint, even to consider the possibility of the resurrection's veracity is absurd. No possible or conceivable evidence could prove it. It is almost impossible to argue with this dogmatic mindset because it has become the supreme, unquestioned standard by which every argument is tested and to which every opinion must conform. This modern view of reality is thoroughly naturalistic, its secularism so powerfully fixed in the minds of its adherents that there appears to be no possibility for them to reconsider restoring the supernatural to human thought by asking whether the resurrection is true. It is useless for modernists to consider any evidence for the resurrection other than to expose how such evidence can be accounted for in purely naturalistic terms.

All of us can identify in a measure with this secular mindset because we are deeply rooted in and shaped by it. The reality of a transcendent God and the role of the supernatural have receded farther and farther away in our experience as we live by the expanding, all-embracing hypotheses, discoveries, and amazing achievements and enormous successes of the scientific endeavor. As a result, as Christians in the modern world, many of us live with the uneasiness of a profound and conflicting dualism. On the one hand we live our practical, everyday life in a secularized world with the limiting, naturalistic perspectives of its *Zeitgeist*. But on the other hand we seek to live in commitment to the Christian faith, embracing supernaturalism with its mysteries of the Triune God, creation and providence, miracles, the incarnation and resurrection, substitutionary atonement and divine forgiveness, prayer and divine healing, life after death, the return of Christ and prophecies of a new heaven and earth. These beliefs are what give meaning and direction to our lives as Christians and address the fundamental needs of human existence. Our uneasiness arises because of the seemingly insurmountable difficulty of integrating these contradictory views of reality into one worldview, making it possible for us to live intelligently and with integrity.

It is beyond the intent of this book to discuss the conflict of science and religion and its fractious history in recent centuries, or delve deeply into the philosophical metaphysics of naturalism that shapes the modern mind, were I even competent to do so. I would point out, however, that the twentieth century opened with supreme confidence that science had won the day and would give the world a century of unparalleled progress on every front. In exuberant optimism Victor Hugo's prophecy is now legendary. He predicted that in the twentieth century war would die, the scaffold would die, hatred would die, frontier boundaries would die, dogmas would die, but the human race would live. Was any prophet ever more wrong? It was also predicted that within the century religion would be dead save for dying remnants clinging to their ebbing life. But the century also brought global wars, oppressive and murderous regimes, economic depression and massive starvation, untold misery and suffering from hardships and diseases, unimaginable horrors of man's inhumanity to man, and science perverted to create massive destruction and potential global devastation. Thus in today's turbulent world we are beginning to question the consequences of some of the successes of the modern mind and its competence to deal with our pressing problems as individuals and in society. The appeal of naturalism as a philosophical basis for the living of our lives has been tarnished, and its inadequacies have discredited its relevance to our needs. Perhaps it is not surprising then that the twentieth century has also witnessed an amazing renascence of religions and their role in the world, and a serious mistrust of science and its competence to solve the basic problems of human existence. It may be argued that the twenty-first century has opened with religion once again occupying a significant role in history. It is also true that naturalism is waging its continual battle for dominance in society. In America, under the guise of separation of church and state, it is fighting its battle by seeking to remove all evidences of our religious heritage by legal and judicial means. I recently heard one of its advocates objecting to any public tolerance of Christmas and Easter as an attempt to return to the Dark Ages! In my lifetime it has largely succeeded in secularizing Western Europe and Canada and is aggressively seeking the same in the United

States. Yet as the new century opens there are voices pointing out that secularism is in decline. In the March 2005 issue of *First Things* Paul C. Vitz wrote an article entitled "Psychology in Recovery," in which he said:

> . . . a major theoretical reason for the scaling back of psychology's early and unseemly hubris has been the decline of the secular ideal itself. Today we are witnessing startling growth in Christianity in the U.S. and throughout much of the world. Within Judaism, Orthodoxy has grown vigorously both in Israel and in the U.S. All around the world, secularism is withering. (p. 21)

It has been one of the fascinating and encouraging experiences of my adult life after more than sixty years to observe this shift in the intellectual ferment of our times from the dominance and arrogance of secularism to a new openness to religion and spiritual values.

I believe it is imperative to challenge the purely rationalist mindset that categorically denies the possibility of the resurrection of Jesus and the viability of Christianity. In opposing this modern-day powerful, confident, intolerant, secular mindset, it seems to me, there are two avenues of response. *First, we should expose naturalism's inadequacy to account for the whole of reality, human history, and the totality of our fundamental life experiences, thereby calling into question its dogmatic, naturalistic assumptions.* This is the purpose of this chapter. *Secondly, we must confront this Zeitgeist with the monumental evidences in history for the resurrection with its enormous consequences that cannot, I believe, be adequately accounted for within the limits of naturalism. The Easter event constitutes a tremendously important factor that demands a reasonable explanation beyond naturalism.*

To consider in depth the inadequacies of the secular mindset to account for the whole of reality, I defer to the learned and competent philosophers and theologians who have exposed them. Although naturalism is as old as Democritus, it arose as an explicit philosophy with the Enlightenment and shaped the modern worldview based on science that has no place for the supernatural and discredits any experience that purports to establish the supernatural. George F. Thomas, in his *Religious Philosophies of the West*,[1] says the limitations of naturalism ultimately

> ... rest upon a dogmatic and arbitrary restriction of knowledge to that which can be discovered and verified by the scientific method. There is no valid reason for accepting this absolutization of the scientific method. It results from the fact that natural science has had remarkable success in describing the phenomena of the natural world and has enabled technology to further man's welfare and comfort. But it does not provide us with knowledge of all aspects and dimensions of reality. ... it cannot account for the purposiveness and organization of living organisms or the intellectual and moral activity of persons. Of course, life and mind are embodied and have physical manifestations which science can investigate by its method, but this does not mean that their unique characteristics and capacities can be exhaustively known by the scientific method. Hence the attempt to exalt that method by denying the value of all other methods is simply an example of "methodological imperialism" and the intellectual pride that leads to it. (p. 347)

Naturalism, in fact, cannot account for very basic aspects of existence, as William Ernest Hocking, in his *Types of Philosophy*,[2] points out: "If I am right in thinking that the strong side of Naturalism is the completeness of its explanations, it becomes vulner-

---

1. New York: Charles Scribner's Sons, 1965.
2. New York: Scribner's, 1929.

able at once if at any point its explanations are incomplete and *necessarily* so" (p. 94). He goes on to ask, "Is there any such point?" He proceeds to enumerate such points in his judgment: experienced qualities such as color, sound, odors, tastes, and touch; and especially the mind (which cannot be equated with the brain) that deals with qualities, values, morals, meaning, pleasures and pain, and particularly itself. Hocking calls attention to "Pascal's observation of the greatness and littleness of the human being. As compared with the mountain, man is minute; the mountain may crush him. But man (in so far as he is a mind) has this point of superiority, he knows he is being crushed, whereas the mountain does not know of its own superiority. As knower of the infinity of the universe of nature, man is the greater thing" (p. 98). This is in contrast to naturalism's dismissal of humans and their history as accidental, meaningless aberrations in the vast universe, as insignificant in the sum total of things as foam on a mug of beer.

In the July 4, 2005, issue of *Newsweek* magazine, George Will, writing about the Scopes trial, comments on today's intelligent design theory: "The problem with intelligent design theory is not that it is false but that it is not falsifiable: Not being susceptible to contradicting evidence, it is not a testable hypothesis. Hence it is not a scientific but a creedal tenet — a matter of faith, unsuited to a public school's science curriculum." I would respond by pointing out that intelligent design assumes a Mind is responsible for the design, and the existence of that Mind can be neither proved or disproved. But if there is no possible way for science to explain the design, it is not inappropriate for the public school to posit the possibility of a Mind. The mystery of human minds is an integral part of any history class.

Indeed, I believe, there are hosts of fundamental and crucial unknowns that invalidate naturalism as an all-embracing worldview. Are there not innumerable non-historical realities that are inaccessible to historical scrutiny and yet produce observable historical events? History and culture are full of events whose origination is beyond naturalism's inquiry. The musical genius of Mozart, the creativity of Shakespeare, the artistic genius of Michelangelo, the versatility of Leonardo da Vinci, the probing mind of Einstein, the religious genius of the Buddha, all of whose efforts are accessible to historical research but whose originating genius is inaccessible to science. Are there not ". . . multiple instances of artists, and poets, and mystics, and lovers, and parents, whose 'effects' are obvious and well-known but whose 'causes' remain inaccessible to historical inquiry?"[3] There are many *supranatural* elements, in the sense of "beyond naturalism," that find expression in reality, in addition to what Christians believe are *supernatural* realities, in the sense of "above naturalism," as is the Triune God.

This inadequacy of naturalism can be illustrated, I believe, from two parables of its defenders designed to illumine how science has effectively eliminated belief in the supernatural world and the existence of God by successfully accounting for reality in naturalistic terms. One is Franz Kafka's story of the castle. The setting of the parable is from feudal days, when serfs lived around a castle set on the mountain in which lives the lord of the fiefdom. In the parable the serfs have lived in the shadow of the castle with its presumed lord for many years although they have never seen him, nor heard from him, nor had any tangible evidence of his presence in and around the castle. They nonetheless continue to believe and assume that the lord to whom they owe their allegiance inhabits the castle, until some skeptics question whether there is in fact such a Lord in the castle. A party of serfs ascend the hill to search the castle to verify the presence or absence of the lord. The party finds the castle empty. This, according to Kafka, describes the experience of modern man, who has always believed in God until now in modern times it is evident he does not exist. There is no lord of the fiefdom. We may assume the serfs are free to live without any allegiance and loyalty, any purpose or meaning beyond their own creation.

3. Luke Timothy Johnson, *The Real Jesus* (San Francisco: Harper, 1996), p. 140.

My response to Kafka is simple: Who built the castle? What is the meaning of its presence, and what accounts for it? Was it built with no purpose? Did it have no builder? It was obviously not a minor factor in the lives of the serfs. Applying the parable as Kafka intended to our modern situation, we are left with something unexplained — the presence of the castle — that has enormous implications for our existence beyond the competence of Naturalism to answer. Secular scientific methods leave vital, basic questions regarding the origin, meaning, and purpose of reality unanswered. Is there no Creator? Is the universe without purpose and our existence without meaning? What accounts for our craving for meaning and purpose in life? What explains our moral sensitivity and concerns? To question the reality of causation, as Hume and others have done, so flies in the face of our common and innate experience that it defies the universality of human reasoning and experience. Its arguments are about as satisfying as the arguments for solipsism, which holds that nothing exists or is real but the individual self. The unknowns so integral to understanding human existence multiply, unanswered by Naturalism.

A second parable designed to illustrate how secularism has eliminated God and the supernatural from life is from Anthony Flew, a British philosopher who is quoted in Paul M. Van Buren's *The Secular Meaning of the Gospel:*

> Once upon a time two explorers came upon a clearing in the jungle. In the clearing were growing many flowers and many weeds. One explorer says, "Some gardener must tend this plot." The other disagrees. "There is no gardener." So they pitch their tents and set a watch. No gardener is ever seen. "But perhaps he is an invisible gardener." So they set up a barbed wire fence. They electrify it. They patrol with bloodhounds. But no shrieks ever suggest that some intruder has received a shock. No movement of the wire ever betrays an invisible climber. The bloodhounds never give cry. Yet still

the Believer is not convinced. "But there is a gardener, invisible, intangible, insensible to electric shocks, a gardener who has no scent and makes no sound, a gardener who comes secretly to look after the garden which he loves." At last the Skeptic despairs. "But what is left of your original assertion? Just how does what you call an invisible, intangible, eternally elusive gardener differ from an imaginary gardener or even from no gardener at all?" Flew concludes, "A fine brash hypothesis may thus be killed by inches, the death of a thousand qualifications."[4]

To this I would respond: ask the Skeptic what accounts for the plot of flowers and weeds? Does not the existence of the plot indicate some meaning, some purpose, some planning, some causation not available to his methods of verification? To conclude the plot is merely a chance happening in the woods is incompatible with the innate demands of the human mind for rational thinking in terms of causes and effects, purpose and meaning; the same inherent rationality the Skeptic has employed to eliminate the gardener in the parable. The Skeptic is left with a fundamental unknown — the existence of the plot of flowers and weeds — beyond the competence of his naturalism to explain.

Just recently, the *Christian Century* of January 11, 2005, carried an intriguing update to this discussion.

Anthony Flew, 81, a British philosopher who has long championed atheism, had changed his mind about the existence of God, at least in a limited way. "I do not believe in the God of any revelatory system, although I am open to that," Flew told the journal of the Evangelical Philosophical Society, *Philosophia Christi*. Flew, a prolific writer, first disclosed his new views in a discussion with several others at New York

4. New York: Macmillan, 1963, p. 3.

University organized by the Institute for Metascientific Research. "I think that the more impressive arguments [for God] are those supported by recent scientific discoveries," he said, even contending that the argument for "intelligent design" is "enormously stronger than it was when I first met it." (p. 15)

Carl E. Braaten, in his Introduction to Pinchas Lapide's *The Resurrection of Jesus: A Jewish Perspective,*[5] updates us on Van Buren:

> Paul Van Buren, one of the so-called Death of God theologians of the sixties, wrote the obituary of God in his book *The Secular Meaning of the Gospel.* His latest book, *Discerning the Way,* is a sketch of a theology of the Jewish Christian reality and represents a 180-degree reversal of position, wherein he recants the secular nonsense he wrote about God in his earlier treatise. In his latest book he speaks of God, not in some newly discovered secular sense, but in a biblical sense. "The Bible," he says, "recalls to us the God who has ever dealt with His creatures in historical, temporal fashion, not as an Absolute outside of history and time."

It is significant to note that as Alfred North Whitehead developed his process philosophy, a modern theoretic ontology, his vision of reality based on modern science in which the matter/ spirit (brain/mind) division with its problems is surmounted by their unity in all "entities," he was driven to posit God within the relationships of his system, much to the chagrin of his atheist associates. Some have attempted to show that the concept of God is not necessary to the Whiteheadian position, "but most commentators would disagree vehemently, insisting (I think cor-

5. Minneapolis: Augsburg, 1983, p. 27.

rectly) that without the concept of God the whole system falls into ruin."[6] It is the nature of God "as persuasive love who educes from this world the response which moves it towards greater sharing in his love . . . hence towards the fuller realization of his purpose — a purpose which is the greatest possible participation of everything in that love" (p. 36). Whitehead was forced to move beyond naturalism to a naturalism with a "built-in supernaturalism" to account for the whole of reality.

The current debate about the evidence for "intelligent design" focuses on the question of whether, in addition to causes operative in the universe, there is also purpose involved. Or to put it in more technical language: in addition to causality, is there also teleology in the structure of the universe? Causality works from the past to the present; teleology works from the future to the present. The question is, if we have a world in which everything is within the causal order, must we dismiss the idea that there is purpose in it? W. E. Hocking in his *Types of Philosophy*[7] has pointed out

> . . . that the naturalistic believer in [emergent evolution] relies on causality alone; and in doing so makes use of an unavowed assumption, namely, that changes of form being implied in the constant motion of the ingredients of the world, given sufficient time all possible forms must be arrived at, all possible arrangements of the ultimate units of the world, so that eventually organisms were bound to happen. . . . [But] the assumption on which the naturalistic emergentist relies is unfounded: form has no inherent tendency to rise. If it does rise, it is as if the series of shapes which constitute the causal history of the universe were selected from an infi-

6. Norman Pittenger, "Alfred North Whitehead," in *Makers of Contemporary Theology* (Cambridge: Lutterworth Press, 1969), p. 34.

7. New York: Scribner's, 1929.

nite number of possible other shapes. And the grounds required for applying the idea of purpose are present. Emer-
gent evolution is as if it were the result of intention. . . . To
take the argument at its minimum showing, it is possible
that there is in the world something more than nature, —
namely, a purpose which the configuration of this nature of
ours obeys. With this possibility the force of naturalism is
broken. (cf. pp. 107-16)

J. Edward Carothers, a process theologian, has written a book
from his perspective on the concept of God entitled *The Pusher
and the Puller*[8] from "data clustering around the doctrine of the
evolutionary process" that denotes purpose in the universe (p. 8).
Is not the science of history constantly hampered by the mysteries of the human mind? Is it surprising that the traces of intelligent design are solved not by the addition of eons of time for their
explanations, but by the mysteries of a divine Mind? "Who has
known the mind of the Lord? Or who has been his counselor?
Who has given a gift to him, to receive a gift in return? For from
him and through him and to him are all things. To him be the
glory forever. Amen" (Romans 11:34-36).

An exchange between Henry Nelson Wieman, the self-styled
religious naturalist from the mid-twentieth century, and Reinhold
Niebuhr bears on the same issue of the inadequacy of naturalism
to embrace the whole of reality. Niebuhr reflects on this exchange:[9]

The trouble with religious naturalism is not only that it obscures the whole mystery of the divine, the mystery of creativity and grace, but that it also falsifies the whole drama of

8. Nashville: Abingdon, 1968.
9. *Reinhold Niebuhr: His Religious, Social, and Political Thought,* ed. Charles W.
Kegley and Robert W. Bretall (New York: Macmillan, 1956), pp. 447-49.

human history with its increasing heights of good and evil and in the paradoxical relation of persons to this drama. For persons are both the creatures and the creators of the process. Professor Wieman is under the impression that a classical Christian faith is merely a crude, pre-scientific way of looking at the world, God, and the self. He, with the help of modern science and the ontology of Dewey and Whitehead (more Dewey than Whitehead) . . . will construct a more adequate view of God and the world. He will define either the temporal process itself as God, or that part of it which is value-creating.

No one could deny that this picture of the self and of God, of the world and of history is more "rational" than the Christian picture in the sense that its coherences are neater and its mystery had been abolished from the realm of meaning, the latter being reduced to rational intelligibility on the lowest level of a scientific account of "nature."

The only trouble with the picture is that all significant truths and facts about man and God, about the nobility and the misery of human freedom, and about the judgment and mercy of God, are left out of the picture. Thus a culture which prides itself on its "empiricism" obscures and denies every "fact" which does not fit into its frame of meaning. The frame of meaning is determined on the one hand by the concept of "nature" or the "temporal process," and on the other hand by the so-called "scientific method" which ironically enough is meant to ascertain the "facts." Unfortunately, there are some "facts" which escape the "method." The irrationality of this cult of "reason" is that it denies the reality of any fact which does not fit into the conception of rational coherence.

The inadequacy of naturalism, explicit in all the above, is its view of reality without purpose and our existence as meaningless because these factors are beyond science to discover. Naturalism does not acknowledge the presence of an innate need for meaning in human consciousness. In my judgment this leaves the naturalist with a huge unknown at the very core of her interpretation of our existence and the universe in which we live and have our being. The naturalist employs her mind with its reasoning power to deny the existence of transcendence but meanwhile ignores the same mind's innate need for meaning and purpose that is fundamental to rational living. Do not scientists require the presupposition that the universe as a whole is rational in all its parts for them to do science? Does not such rationality imply there is meaning in history, a purpose in the universe to which all its parts contribute?

How shall we live in this dismal predicament of meaninglessness, according to the naturalists? Jean Paul Sartre, the famous atheistic, existentialist philosopher of the post–World War II era in France, having concluded that human existence is meaningless, recognized that nonetheless humans have a fundamental need for meaning and purpose in their lives, and so he proposed they live as a man in a small rowboat on the ocean in a pitch dark night: light a lantern, place it on the prow of the boat and row toward it. That is, Sartre's advice was for humans to create personal and temporary meanings, purposes, and goals and pursue them so we can live life with some direction and satisfaction. But how viable is naturalism as a philosophy when it cannot account for what is most inherently a part of ourselves as humans? How can we live by a worldview that leads to denying that it is livable?

After World War II, Victor Frankl, a Jewish psychiatrist who survived the Holocaust but lost almost his entire family in the unbelievable suffering and death in the prison camps, developed his theory of logotherapy. From his harrowing experience in the camps he observed that those victims who possessed a *will to meaning* in their lives had a better chance to survive. According to logotherapy, the striving to find a meaning in one's life is the primary motivational force in humanity — not meaning we invent on our own, but meaning we detect. They are values that do not push but pull us, and which we have the freedom to choose to fulfill or forfeit. Meaning in life is a fundamental and necessary component of human existence that naturalism totally ignores.

Recently I read the obituary of Pierre Victor, a Frenchman who died in June 2004. It is reported that he had been instrumental in the conversion of Jean-Paul Sartre from his atheistic existentialism shortly before his death. Sartre, who throughout his mature career was a militant atheist, in his last months in 1980 wrote in an exchange with Victor in the *Nouvel Observateur,* "I do not feel that I am the product of chance, a speck of dust in the universe, but someone who was expected, prepared, prefigured. In short, a being whom only a Creator could put here: and this idea of a creating hand refers to God."[10] Students of atheistic existentialism will note that in this one sentence Sartre disavowed the entire system that engaged his life.

Throughout reality we see causes, dependent relationships, interlocking purposes, and meaningful connections. All are essential to make rational living possible — and, I may add, have given through the ages great plausibility to the teleological argument for God's existence. The naturalist flies in the face of these evidences in her dogged commitment to the scientific method, lest she find herself driven to the high probability of a supernaturalism that gives meaning and purpose to existence. This is the fatal dilemma: human existence cries out for purpose and meaning, but naturalism has no place for these basic demands of existence.

~

For the religious naturalist, belief in the resurrection of Jesus is totally incredible, yet it also creates a dilemma. In his book *The*

10. *The National Review,* June 11, 1982, p. 677.

Reality of the Resurrection,[11] Merrill C. Tenney describes this dilemma:

> The artless straightforward narrative of the resurrection of Christ in the Gospels presents a difficult dilemma for modern thought. If, in order to avoid acceptance of a miracle which would be embarrassing to the normative principles of science, its genuineness be rejected, the whole structure of Christian truth degenerates into a superstition containing at best an insecure modicum of ethical principles. If, on the other hand, the fact be freely admitted as an article of faith, the naturalistic interpretation of the world must be discarded. Can the Gospels be taken as accurate historical reports, or are they idealized projections of theological teaching, stated in cultural terms which are no longer relevant? Or do they embody a truth which cannot be expressed adequately by the language of any culture, but which, on the other hand, cannot be explained away by any intellectual device? (p. 186)

This basic dilemma is also recognized by the more liberal New Testament scholar Reginald H. Fuller in the opening sentences of his book *The Formation of the Resurrection Narratives:*[12]

> Clearly, the New Testament asserts that something over and above the Good Friday event happened in the experience of the first disciples, something more than their coming to a new assessment of the meaning of the event of Good Friday. Even the most skeptical historian has to postulate an "x" as M. Dibelius called it, to account for the complete change in the behavior of the disciples, who at Jesus' arrest had fled

11. New York: Harper and Row, 1963.
12. New York: Macmillan, 1971, pp. 1-2.

and scattered to their own homes, but who in a few weeks were found boldly preaching their message to the very people who had sought to crush the movement launched by Jesus by disposing of its leader.

What is the precise content of the "x"? What really happened at Easter? Can the historian go any farther than leaving it as an insoluble problem? The New Testament itself is quite clear on what the "x" was: the tomb of Jesus was discovered empty on Easter Sunday morning, and Jesus appeared to his disciples as one risen from the dead.

Marc Bloch in his *The Historian's Craft*[13] explains that basic to the whole historical inquiry is the estimation that "the universe and society possess sufficient uniformity to exclude the possibility of overly pronounced deviations." Therefore the historian as a scientist has no room for such an "overly pronounced deviation" as the miracle of the resurrection. To allow for the miracle of the resurrection presupposes factors beyond the uniformity of nature — factors that threaten the possibility of scientific history.

The science of history, according to Bloch, is the attempt to provide knowledge about the activities of men who lived in the past. He asserts that the only means for gaining this knowledge are the tracks humans leave behind, and these tracks are of two kinds: the intentional and the unintentional. The intentional include such elements as a written record of things that happened. They are essential in providing a chronological framework without which an understanding of history is impossible. The disadvantage of intentional sources is that writers have recorded the subject matter in a way that they wish it to be seen. Their reporting may be biased and slanted to fit their perception of an event, and the historian must take such factors into consideration. That is certainly true of the Gospels in the New Testament. All the au-

13. Manchester: University Press, 1967.

thors write from the unambiguous premise that the resurrection was an event that happened at a specific time and in a specific place. They were no impartial reporters, but sincere and committed propagandists to further the Christian cause, which appears to undermine their value for historical research, though (and this is important) it leaves the question how and why they became propagandists for the Christian faith. That is the "x" that confounds the historian.

The unintentional tracks for the historian are everything left from the past indicating how people lived and behaved. They are valuable because they were left unintentionally and are not colored by an intermediate storyteller. But studying the unintentional tracks is extremely difficult. The historian must study humanity indirectly through the medium of these tracks, which makes the results of the study constantly subject to new information, new approaches, new hypotheses of interpretation, and the like. In this study of the unintentional tracks the scientific historian is restricted by the assumption that eliminates miracles as a possible factor in explaining the past, so the data that appear to have resulted from the resurrection are problematic. The historian must seek to find reasonable, naturalistic explanations for the unintentional tracks that confront her in the existence of the Christian church, in the Epistles and Gospels of the New Testament, in the astonishing changes within Judaism that gave rise to Christianity. If the resurrection as a supernatural event cannot be an option in interpreting the unintentional tracks, the historian is left with an inescapable unknown of tremendous significance for the interpretation of history.

On the other hand, Bloch contends, the unity of the universe and human behavior cannot be so uniform that the unexpected and the surprising cannot happen, because human nature includes the peculiarities of individuals and their "free will" to behave in unexpected and unpredictable ways, which is precisely the subject matter of history. Nature (weather, earthquakes, pestilence, and hereditary factors) does affect the course of history, but human behavior in response to its environment is the mainspring of history. The existence and history of Christianity is the crucial story of human behavior in response to what purports to have been a totally new phenomenon in nature: the resurrection of a dead person into a new form of existence. The insularity of that phenomenon might well exclude it from historical exploration, but not necessarily as a possible explanation for the rise of the unknown in history. Does not the unexplainable reality of "free will" — an unknown — within scientific history also leave room for the possibility of some other operative "will" beyond historical exploration, but that is nonetheless active in human history? The historian as historian can go no further than acknowledging the existence of these unknowns. He cannot affirm on the basis of his science the possibility of a supernatural intrusion in history to explain the resurrection, but neither can he deny its possibility on the basis of his science.

Obviously the truth of the resurrection cannot be verified by scientific historians because it is outside the scope and authority of scientific historiography. *But it is also likewise outside the competence of historians to declare the supernatural nonexistent.* Peter Hamilton, a process theologian who does not accept the bodily resurrection of Jesus, comments in his book, *The Living God and the Modern World:*[14]

> Those who regard the accounts of the empty tomb and its sequel as incredible, and a great stumbling block to the faith of "modern man," should pause to reflect that it is impossible to disprove these accounts, except in so far as they conflict with each other.
>
> One can affirm that the unique events never occur, but this is an assumption: it cannot be proved without a knowl-

14. Philadelphia: The United Church Press, 1967.

edge of every single event that has ever occurred. Those who believe in God as living and, in some sense, transcendent would presumably attribute at least some uniqueness to God: it cannot be impossible that a unique God should sometimes act uniquely. One may think the unique event of a visible Resurrection unlikely: one may feel that a faith that depends upon such an event is weaker than one that does not, but one ought not to maintain that the traditional interpretation of Christ's Resurrection is impossible. (pp. 214-15)

The fact is that science has nothing to say about the truth of the resurrection, and thus for philosophical naturalism that rests on scientific methodology to deny the possibility of the resurrection is an unwarranted and gratuitous assumption.

Throughout the years numerous hypotheses based *on purely naturalistic grounds* were and are proposed to account for the rise of the Easter phenomenon in history and the existence of the church that claims to be founded on the resurrection of Christ. There is no unanimity of opinion among these speculative hypotheses. Their primary purpose is to render plausible alternatives to the miracle of the resurrection with its powerful witness as the *sine qua non* of Christianity. They have a long history. The earliest appears in the Gospel of Matthew (28:11-15), where we are told the story was circulated among the Jews that the disciples stole the body of Jesus from the tomb while the guards were asleep. The existence of the story is, of course, an implicit admission that the tomb was empty.[15] Joseph Klausner, in his *Jesus of Nazareth*,[16] proposed that Joseph of Arimathea secretly removed the body of Jesus and buried it in an unknown grave (p. 357). But Klausner does not explain why Joseph did not inform the disciples when the news of

---

15. Cf. Ethelbert Stauffer's *Jesus and His Story* (New York: Knopf, 1974), pp. 143-47.

16. New York: Knopf, 1960.

Jesus' resurrection was announced, particularly since he was one of them. Celsus, an early opponent of Christianity, supposed the story of the resurrection was due to the hysteria of women. An early Enlightenment critic, Hermann S. Reimarus, suggested that the disciples, once having enjoyed the easy life as pupils of Jesus, decided to promote the story of his resurrection so they might continue the lifestyle to which they had grown accustomed — totally ignoring the price they paid of sacrificing their lives for the story. How desperate and ridiculous some critics become in search for a naturalistic solution to the unknown!

Popular writers as well as scholars have entered the fray, proposing speculations covering the spectrum from the absurd conclusion that the entire story of Jesus — his life, death, and resurrection — is a myth, to more fanciful scenarios such as Barbara Thiering's *Jesus and the Riddle of the Dead Sea Scrolls.*[17] She proposes that Jesus was buried in a cave; he didn't actually die; and he was revived by the magician Simon Magnus, after which he married Mary Magdalene, had three children, was later divorced and finally died in Rome. This wild speculation has been incorporated into Dan Brown's best-selling novel *The Da Vinci Code.*[18] Morton Smith writes that Jesus was a practicing homosexual and conjuror. The German scholar Gerd Ludemann calls the resurrection an empty formula that must be rejected by anyone holding a scientific worldview (as if the ancients did not know that dead people never return to life). G. A. Wells held that the name "Jesus" is empty, like "Santa Claus," and doesn't trace back to or denote anyone at all. John Allegro seems to think there was no such person as Jesus of Nazareth; Christianity began as a hoax designed to fool the Romans and preserve the cult of a certain hallucinogenic mushroom *(Amanita muscaria).* He believed the name "Christ" is really the name of the mushroom. Another claim is that Jesus was,

17. New York: HarperCollins, 1992.
18. New York: Doubleday, 2003.

in fact, an atheist. Apart from these extremes, Van Harvey is correct in saying, "So far as the biblical historian is concerned . . . there is scarcely a popularly held traditional belief about Jesus that is not regarded with considerable skepticism." (I am indebted in part to Alvin Plantinga's *Warranted Christian Belief*[19] for some of this summary.)

Among scholars who reject the resurrection, perhaps the most popular hypothesis is that somehow in the tormented, guilt-ridden, inconsolable mind of Peter after the shattering experience of his betrayal of Jesus and the horror of his beloved teacher's excruciating, unjust crucifixion, there arose the conviction that he must still be alive. The Jesus he knew and loved and respected so highly could not really be dead! The conviction of Peter's disturbed mind finally produced "visions" of his presence and somehow he convinced other disciples that Jesus was alive, for he had seen him. I first read this proposed solution in Pierre Van Paassen's *Why Jesus Died*[20] and later in Paul M. Van Buren's *The Secular Meaning of the Gospel.*[21] In 1974 the liberal Dominican theologian Edward Schillebeeckx published a large book about Jesus wherein he devoted considerable space to the resurrection, with the same hypothesis. Again the rise of the resurrection myth centered in especially Peter's wonderful experience of grace and forgiveness, of "seeing" and "enlightenment" that can be described as "conversion." According to N. T. Wright,

> Schillebeeckx's entire construct, in fact, is mistaken and misleading . . . at the level of plausible historical reconstruction. It is revealing that when he sums up what he really thinks happened, in perhaps less guarded mode than usual, his position threatens to collapse back into a variation of Al-

19. New York: Oxford University Press, 2000, pp. 400-401.
20. New York: Dial Press, 1949.
21. New York: Macmillan, 1960.

bert Schweitzer: Jesus was a noble but disastrous failure, but his followers were challenged to a new way by the memory of what he did and said. God must have the last word, despite the "historical fiasco" of Jesus, and this the early Christians try to express with their creedal affirmation of Jesus' resurrection — an affirmation whose wording "may be subjected to criticism," by which Schillebeeckx seems to mean that it leads one toward a "crude and naïve realism," the unfortunate belief that something actually happened at Easter. But as we have seen, the historical study of early Christian practice and hope leaves us no choice but to conclude that this unfortunate belief was what all early Christians held. Indeed, they professed that it was the very centre of their life.[22]

No proposed naturalistic interpretation adequately deals with the evidence. Some scholars honestly acknowledge the insoluble mystery. Years ago Charles R. Brown, former professor at Union Theological Seminary in New York, wrote that having considered all the evidence for the resurrection and all the attempts to give a naturalistic explanation for it, he concluded that the best we can do is place the resurrection on a shelf with other unexplained events in history, such as the uncertainty about Shakespeare and the composition of his dramas. Others simply accept the unknown and move on without further comment, as for example Will Durant, in his *The Story of Civilization,* Volume III entitled *Caesar and Christ,*[23] when he simply states without further comment on page 574: "The Master went as mystically as he had come, but most of the disciples seem to have been sincerely convinced that he had, after his crucifixion,

22. *The Resurrection of the Son of God* (Minneapolis: Augsburg Fortress, 2003), pp. 701-6.

23. New York: Simon and Schuster, 1944.

been with them in the flesh." For those commentators who accept the unknown of the Resurrection without further comment, the assumption seems to be that whatever its explanation, it cannot be a miracle. That would require a supernatural world, which in turn would run counter to the fundamental commitments of historical science.

In this connection a comment from Wolfhart Pannenberg, the distinguished post-Barthian, post-Bultmann German scholar, published in the 2005 September/October issue of *Books and Culture,* is pertinent. He was asked, "In what ways have your views on [the actual historical resurrection of Jesus] changed over the years?" To which Pannenberg responded,

There has been no reason to change my views actually. The various alternative explanations with regard to the Christian Easter tradition strike me as less plausible than the biblical accounts themselves. I used to tell my students that you have to study the biblical texts critically, as you study other historical documents. But please, be also critical of the critics. There are too many students who simply accept their teachers' authority, especially when they are so bold and critical with regard to the biblical texts. So I prefer to be critical of the critics. Sometimes, alternative reconstructions are almost ridiculous.

I have never understood how, at Jerusalem, the place of Jesus' crucifixion, a Christian congregation could be established a few weeks after that event, proclaiming his resurrection, without firmly and truly being assured about the fact that the tomb was empty. Of course, critics have different explanations for that fact. But, with regard to the tomb of Jesus being empty, the Christian proclamation couldn't have persisted one day in Jerusalem if that were not the case. I often wonder why there are so many scholars whose imagination doesn't permit them to acknowledge this.

With the denial of the facticity of the resurrection the Enlightenment shifted attention away from the crucifixion and resurrection of Jesus to the life and teachings of Jesus that, it was judged, constitute the true gospel and ground of the church. The example of Jesus' life of love and grace was said to be the gospel that should be emulated in the lives of those who recognized in Jesus a Christ of faith, whose spirit inspires us to lives of dedicated grace and service, as other great religious leaders have taught. Never mind that critical philosophers like Bertrand Russell in his *Why I Am Not a Christian*[24] and Walter Kaufmann in his *The Faith of a Heretic*[25] were not impressed with the nobility of Jesus' teachings or their propriety as norms for our ethical living.

Several consequences of great importance have followed this shift of interest from the resurrection to the life and teachings of Jesus. First, it gave rise to the crucial and inescapable riddle of how the "Jesus of History" became the "Christ of Faith." As we have already noted, Schweitzer's *Quest* is the classic, historical survey of the Jesus of History movement from the beginning of the Enlightenment to the early days of the twentieth century, but it also highlighted the inexplicable rise of the Christ of Faith that inspired Schweitzer to his personal story of dedicated service and sacrifice. A second result was that, with the emphasis on the historical life of Jesus and the belief that it was inconceivable that a dead man should rise again, there was a loss of interest in the Easter accounts in the Gospels. They were dismissed as an inconsequential, confusing mythic conclusion to the life of Jesus that evolved in the pre-scientific days of early Christianity. Therefore much liberal theology and literature simply ignored the resurrection. For agnostics like Russell and Kaufmann belief in the resurrection is so preposterous they barely mention it, let alone bother to refute it. There was a period when few serious books were writ-

24. London: Watts, 1927.
25. Garden City, N.Y.: Doubleday, 1961.

ten about the resurrection, which ended when the rise of neo-orthodoxy highlighted it as the flash point of the divine-human encounter in history. And finally, denying the resurrection inevitably led to the denial of the uniqueness of Christianity as the result of God's divine entrance into human history in Jesus Christ for the salvation of the world. Christianity was equated with the other great religions that arose from the teachings of gifted spiritual founders whose proposed worldviews gave meaning and purpose to human life, offering "salvation" through religious instruction and providing ethical prescriptions to cope with the problems of living and dying. Meanwhile critics lost sight of the fact that the resurrection first of all distinguished Christianity from all the other religions of the world by centering its faith in a living Lord rather than in the teachings of deceased founders.

Naturalism's inability to account for the resurrection highlights the fact that, as a worldview, it is simply riddled with unknowns. It ignores, as Reinhold Niebuhr concluded, all the significant truths about man and God by denying or ignoring any fact which does not fit into its concept of rational coherence. If it cannot account for the details of the resurrection and the formation of the church that proceeded from it, and if it cannot account for so many fundamental realities and experiences of our lives, why should we let it undermine our faith?

✢ IV ✢

"Christ Has Been Raised from the Dead"

———≈———

I t is indisputable that something amazing happened in Palestine in the first century that gave rise to Christianity. The New Testament identifies and reports that happening as a bodily resurrection of the crucified Jesus, as witnessed by his enigmatic but unmistakable appearances to his disciples and other followers and their testimony that the tomb in which he had been buried was empty. There were no witnesses to the actual miracle of the resurrection, only the testimony of witnesses who verified afterwards that they had seen the risen Christ. It is historically verifiable that belief in the resurrection so convinced and empowered these witnesses that their testimony with its results gave rise to the Christian church that spread rapidly throughout the Roman Empire, creating an overwhelming torrent of influential consequences that extend through the centuries to the present day. As Kenneth Scott Latourette puts it:

> One of the most amazing and significant facts of history is that within five centuries of its birth Christianity won the professed allegiance of the overwhelming majority of the population of the Roman Empire and even the support of the Roman state. Beginning as a seemingly obscure sect of

Judaism, one of the scores, even hundreds of religions and religious groups which were competing within the realm, revering as its central figure one who had been put to death by the machinery of Rome, and in spite of having been long proscribed by that government and eventually having the full weight of the state thrown against it, Christianity proved so far the victor that the empire sought alliance with it and to be a Roman citizen became identical with being a Christian.[1]

Such an amazing and improbable history demands a necessary and sufficient cause to account for its existence, expansion, influence, and enduring viability through good times and bad for two thousand years. We are able to review twenty centuries in hindsight to observe and study the checkered history of the church. In our world of good and evil, it is no surprise to find both within its membership. Its demise has been frequently predicted, its devotees ridiculed by a secular intelligentsia and persecuted by hostile governments. The church has been challenged by competing religions, its life betrayed from within by perfidy and hypocrisy and soiled by misuse and abuse. Nonetheless it lives on, some times retreating, often arising with new vitality and expanding power, till there is today no nation without the witness of the church. According to a March 2005 *Newsweek* poll, 81 percent of Americans say they are Christians. They are part of the world's largest faith, with 2 billion believers, or roughly 33 percent of the earth's population. Martin Marty has illustrated the church's phenomenal strength to survive in spite of severe threats with the example of an inflated balloon that, when squeezed in our hands, bulges between our fingers in new and dramatic shapes.

The twentieth century has marvelously illustrated the severe opposition to Christianity by atheistic, totalitarian regimes. Un-

1. *A History of Christianity* (New York: HarperSanFrancisco, 1975), p. 65.

der the impact of secularism, Christianity has declined in the advancing societies of Western Europe, Canada, and the United States to such a degree that many have predicted its death. In 1959, on the centennial of Darwin's *Origin of Species,* Aldous Huxley proudly announced that religion was dead but for a few dying kicks. The secular intelligentsia of Western Europe and the United States were proclaiming in the mid-century that God was dead and the church had no future. I remember in the 1960s a discouraged immigrant minister from the Netherlands, living in Canada, saying to me in no uncertain terms that the church was dead, yes, dead! Throughout the first three quarters of the twentieth century the media generally highlighted the liberal debunking and radical denial of the gospel. But in the last quarter of the century the media has taken notice of the church reviving with new vitality and striking power in the United States and the Southern Hemisphere to spread throughout the world both within and beyond the denominational structures of the church. Some observers claim it has made greater conquests in this period than at any time in its history, employing the advances of modern science and technology in communication and transportation.

The historian must deal not only with the church, but with all the consequences in history that have resulted from its presence. Inseparable from and indispensable for the church is the formation of the New Testament canon, witnessing firsthand to the life, death, and resurrection of Jesus, rooted in the Old Testament revelation and in fulfillment of its promises. Second is the New Testament solution to the major historical riddle of how the crucified Jesus of history became the exalted Christ of Faith for his followers through his resurrection. Third is the otherwise inexplicable impact in history of the fundamental role and place of the Sabbath for the Jews, rooted in their stories of creation and ethnic origins and their identity as God's peculiar people, that was changed to the Christian Sunday as the day for the church's worship because Jesus arose on the first day of the week. The change signified, it was believed, the beginning of the renewed creation, of which Jesus was the firstfruits. Fourth is the explanation of the revolutionary change from the basic Jewish belief as God's chosen people to the inclusive embrace of all peoples in the church whom God loved and for whom Christ died and arose from the dead. Fifth is the explanation for the resources and powers inherent in the gospel of the resurrection that inspired, energized, and molded society and culture to create Western civilization — evidenced, for example, in the worldwide adoption of the division of world history into B.C. and A.D. It is witnessed in the dynamic inspiration of its worldview that cultivates perspectives, principles, and values from the gospel that influence the history of the entire world. Today society throughout the world, including Christianity's greatest critics, are indebted to the gospel for its respect for human life and dignity, the expansion of human freedom, the spread of democracy, concern for the oppressed in society, racial equality, recognition of the equality and dignity of women, opposition to abortion, the end of female infanticide, worldwide compassion and generosity for the poor and deprived, the promotion of universal education, the rise of and support for science and its achievements, medical advances and concerns for health and well-being, the establishment of hospitals, and even the idealism of Socialism and Marxism. Finally, I would note the contagious conviction in the hearts of believers throughout the ages and today of the experience of the living Lord in their lives with his transforming power of faith, hope, and love. This contagion reverberates in every generation, some times more clearly than others, in believers who echo the conviction of St. Paul: "I know whom I have believed" (2 Timothy 1:12), and attribute this continuing power to the presence and activity of Christ in the Holy Spirit.

These results have empowered, shaped, and defined much of Western civilization. But the whole story is that being in the world and society has had a major impact on the church. The church as an institution and witness in society has been influenced, compromised, weakened, diluted, distorted, polluted, fractured, and abused, frequently to the detriment of its virginal testimony in the world. Too often it has become another instrument for oppression and evil in the world — though I believe its fundamental character eventually shines through, exposing its own evil and continuing to bear the inherent power of reform and renewal. All this data of the growth and character, the corruption and renewal of Christianity and its impact on civilization to the present is in the domain of historians, who cannot ignore these historical realities nor their origins. It is the Christian's testimony that the resurrection of Jesus ultimately accounts for the church's dynamic presence with its impact and effect in the world.

It is here that an important distinction in the meaning of *resurrection* must be made. For although some in the liberal circles of the church and many in the world at large do not believe the miracle of the resurrection, there remains a recognition of the importance of the resurrection to account for Christianity. A few years ago I heard a Jewish professor of New Testament from Vanderbilt University in a sermon implore her church audience not to deny or surrender the significance of the resurrection, even though this same professor acknowledged she does not believe in the bodily resurrection of Jesus. She recognized that the concept of resurrection is crucial to the meaning and vitality of Christianity.

Therefore it is very important that we ask: What do Christians believe happened in the resurrection and what does it mean? There are basically two very different interpretations of the Easter event, both claiming to affirm the resurrection. The difference between the two views is carefully defined by G. W. H. Lampe:

This is the question whether what happened on the first Easter was an objective event in the external world or whether it was simply a change of mind, radical and dramatic, but not necessarily sudden, on the part of the disciples. Was the Resurrection an event in the life of Jesus, so that we can say God actually raised him from the dead? Or was it only an event in the lives of the disciples — a change in their outlook as they came to realize through further reflection on their dead and buried Teacher, that his influence lived on, that his teaching had been true, that his life must be their example and his character a pattern for themselves to follow, that although he was dead he must still be revered in their memory as their Lord whose spirit could still be recreated in themselves in so far as they dedicated themselves to the aim of following in his footsteps? When we say that Jesus was raised from the dead are we speaking literally or metaphorically? Do we mean that he was raised in the minds of the disciples: that as they remembered him and began to put a new and higher value on his words and deeds he seemed to be still so real to them and so uniquely important that they found that they could think of him as though he were still with them? Or are we making a factual assertion, not only about the mental processes of the disciples but about Jesus himself? Are we saying that however mysterious and inexplicable the event may be, Jesus was actually alive, in a new and glorious mode of existence, although he had really died and been buried?[2]

Luke Timothy Johnson, in his *Finding God in the Questions,*[3] distinguishes between Christians who believe in the resurrection and those who cannot properly be called Christians because they do not believe in the resurrection, but like Albert Schweitzer are nonetheless devoted "followers of Christ." The former view is

2. G. W. H. Lampe and D. W. MacKinnon, *The Resurrection: A Dialogue* (Philadelphia: Westminster Press, 1966), pp. 29-30.

3. Downers Grove: InterVarsity Press, 2004.

what T. S. Matthew had in mind when he wrote: "The Resurrection was tremendous good news, if true, the best ever reported" because it sheds light on life and death.

The distinction is enormously important. The first option is grounded in the existence of a supernatural world that has impinged into our world with the miracle of the resurrection, having stupendous implications for our lives. The second option normalizes the resurrection in terms of naturalistic explanations, placing Christianity on a level with other world religions. Our commitment to either option is crucial for our understanding of human existence.

Lampe's rejection of the second option is compelling:

> My reason for this is because I find it incredible. All the indications in the Gospel suggest that at the time of the arrest of Jesus the disciples lost all hope and faith in Jesus. They all forsook him and fled, except Peter, and he very soon denied all knowledge of him. Unless something extraordinary happened to convince them that against all their expectations God had reversed his apparent verdict on Jesus, I cannot imagine that they would later on have taken immense risks to assert in public that a man who had been condemned and hanged was no less than God's Messiah. It proved difficult enough to persuade the world that this was so, even when it was proclaimed by men who believed that God had raised him from the dead. Without that belief I think it inconceivable that the first disciples could have even entertained the idea themselves. . . . I cannot think that apart from the Resurrection, a fundamental change of mind on the disciples' part about the true significance of the crucified Jesus is historically probable or that it is sufficient to account for the origin of the Christian Church. The 'Pentecostal' enthusiasm of the disciples arose, not from the reflection about the value of a dead man's deeds and words,

but from the conviction that that man was alive as Lord and Messiah and that they could testify from their experience of actual encounter with him that God had glorified him.[4]

Critics who support the naturalistic explanation believe they find suggestive hints for their position in the scant biblical data of Paul's implication in 1 Corinthians 15:5 that the risen Jesus appeared to Peter *first,* and from the account in John 21 of Peter's restoration. It supposes that the grieving, guilt-stricken mind of Peter because of his betrayal and cowardice gave rise to his post-Easter experience that the Jesus he knew and loved simply could not be dead. This conviction psychologically conditioned him to hallucinate the appearance of Jesus that mentally relieved him with forgiveness and grace. Peter in turn, it is supposed, persuaded his fellow disciples that Jesus was alive and may have thereby psychologically conditioned them to have their own "appearances." But would not the disciples more realistically have thought Peter had lost his sanity under the stress were he to share with them his unbelievable, hallucinatory notion that Jesus was alive? The disciples too knew that dead people never return to life. Is it reasonable to assume all the disciples, in spite of their doubts, were so convinced they were willing to suffer persecution and finally death for the illusions of Peter's mind? I may note the theory ignores the fact that in the same Johannine story Peter appears to have managed his grief and guilt to the point where he decided to return to his previous way of life. He knew those incredible three years with Jesus were over!

The original witnesses were well aware of the seeming impossibility and apparent absurdity of the Christian claim of Jesus' resurrection. The New Testament itself reports the unbelief, doubts, and resistance that arose in the minds of the immediate witnesses. In Matthew 28:17 it is said that when the eleven disciples

4. Lampe and MacKinnon, *The Resurrection,* pp. 30-31.

saw him they worshiped him, "but some doubted." In the twenty-fourth chapter of the Gospel of Luke we are told that when the disciples saw Jesus they thought they saw a ghost (v. 37). And Jesus said to them, "Why are you so troubled, and why do doubts rise in your minds?" (v. 38). And Luke reports that even after Jesus had shown them his hands and feet with the imprint of the nails "they still did not believe it because of joy and amazement" (v. 41). In other words, it was too good to be true. The Gospel of John relates how Thomas stubbornly resisted accepting the disciples' story that they had seen Jesus alive until Jesus appeared to him, inviting him to touch his wounds to verify his living presence (20:24-28). In Acts we are told the reaction Paul received from his sophisticated audience in Athens when he proclaimed that God had raised Jesus from the dead: "When they heard about the resurrection of the dead, some of them sneered, but others said, 'We want to hear you again on this subject'" (17:31-33). Modern doubt about the resurrection is nothing new, nor is pursuing non-miraculous explanations for the phenomenon the witnesses experienced. Already in the Gospel of Matthew we learn of the earliest denial of the resurrection from local leaders: "the disciples came by night and stole the body away" (28:11-15). Nonetheless the apostles and believers of the early Christian church were so overwhelmingly convinced that Jesus had been resurrected, and not simply resuscitated, that they were willing to die for their testimony, as tradition tells us many of them did.

Critics who begin with the scientific dogma that the resurrection is impossible are reduced, in my judgment, to implausible speculations of what might have happened to account for Christianity. Are they not proposing an incredibly flimsy foundation to account for Christianity and its dynamic influence in history and society for two thousand years? In any way can their naturalistic explanations be called a *sufficient and necessary* foundation on which to build the history of the Christian church? The interpretation that Peter was hallucinating and persuaded the other disciples to accept and even share his hallucinations reveals how desperate are the critics when confronted with the miracle of the resurrection; they have no alternative but to latch on to what on the face of it appears an unrealistic, even preposterous, hypothesis. It is far easier to respect the views of those who simply confess that the resurrection is one of the unsolved mysteries of life they cannot answer.

I, with many others, find compelling the testimony for the resurrection in the New Testament from the Apostle Paul in 1 Corinthians 15:3-17:

> For I handed on to you as of first importance what I in turn had received: that Christ died for our sins in accordance with the Scriptures, that he was buried, and that he was raised on the third day in accordance with the Scriptures, and that he appeared to Cephas, then to the twelve. Then he appeared to more than five hundred brothers and sisters at one time, most of whom are still alive, though some have died. Then he appeared to James, then to all the apostles. Last of all, as to someone untimely born, he appeared also to me. . . . If there is no resurrection of the dead, then Christ has not been raised; and if Christ has not been raised, then our proclamation has been in vain and your faith has been in vain. We are even found to be misrepresenting God, for we testified of God that he raised Christ — whom he did not raise if it is true that the dead are not raised. For if the dead are not raised, then Christ has not been raised. If Christ has not been raised, your faith is futile; you are still in your sins.

According to biblical scholars, 1 Corinthians was written by Paul in the spring of 55 in Ephesus, twenty-five years after the Easter event. But in this passage he refers to what he had preached when he first came to Corinth between 50 and 52. At that time he was reporting what he had been taught earlier when he became a Christian, which was probably less than six or seven years after the death and resurrection of Jesus. Already at that time, within less than a decade, the fundamental facts of Christianity were known, preached, and interpreted by the apostles in the light of the Hebrew Scriptures.

It is important to note that Paul provided this witness to the resurrection "unintentionally" — that is, it was not his primary concern to build the case in defense of the resurrection of Christ with all its evidence, but rather to respond to a dispute within the Corinthian church. The dispute arose in Corinth because there were members in the congregation who did not believe in resurrection of the dead, probably because of the Greek belief in the immortality of the soul and its ideal deliverance in death from the negatives of bodily existence. Paul rejects that position as inconsistent with the resurrection of Christ and therefore summarizes for his readers the historical evidence for belief in the resurrection as well as its doctrinal importance for the Christian faith from the Hebrew Scriptures. We need not interpret Paul, therefore, to have given us a complete report of all the evidence for the resurrection that he might have given if that had been his primary purpose. The Gospel of Luke also affirms in 24:34 that the risen Jesus "appeared to Simon" before appearing to all the disciples. Paul also mentions James, the brother of Jesus, who is never mentioned in the Gospel accounts, but who became a believer and leader in the Jerusalem church after the resurrection and whom Paul met on his visit to Jerusalem. For his purpose in 1 Corinthians, Paul did not need to relate all the known appearances of the risen Jesus. He does not mention the appearances to the women at the tomb, or to the men on the way to Emmaus. His silence about these appearances does not warrant the conclusion he did not know of them. Nor does he mention the empty tomb, although he clearly implies it by his emphasis on Jesus having been buried. Obviously if Jesus was buried and raised on the third day, the tomb was empty. What else could the raising mean? Of course

the empty tomb by itself does not prove the resurrection; someone could have removed the body. But an occupied tomb on
Easter morning certainly would have disproven it. It is interesting
that Paul adds the appearance to about 500 believers not mentioned in the Gospels, unless there is an allusion to it in Matthew
28:10. Most of the 500 were still living when Paul wrote to the Corinthians. It has been suggested that Paul is confusing Pentecost
with Easter at this point. But that Jesus appeared to others than
the eleven disciples is evident in Acts 1:21-26, when it was decided
to replace Judas Iscariot in the circle of the twelve apostles. Peter
declared that the person chosen must be a witness to the resurrection, and from among such witnesses two brethren are mentioned: "Joseph called Barsabbas (also known as Justus) and
Matthias." The Gospels nowhere report their sightings of the risen
Jesus, but their mention in Acts does establish that there were
others who witnessed him as risen. Joseph and Matthias may
have been part of the 500, as well as James, the brother of Jesus.
There are more questions that can be asked about the details of
this crucial passage in 1 Corinthians 15, but none of them casts
any doubt on whether Paul believed and proclaimed the historical reality of Jesus, the Christ, being raised bodily from the dead.

Paul is himself a remarkable evidence for the truth of Jesus'
resurrection. From his undisputed letters of Romans, 1 Corinthians, and Galatians, as well as in Acts, we know that Paul was a
loyal and devoted Jew who shortly after the life and death of Jesus
was determined to squelch the schism within Judaism that was
growing rapidly after the reported resurrection of Jesus and the
Pentecost phenomenon. As an astute observer, he was more
aware of the threat of Christianity to Judaism than the learned
Gamaliel. A more unlikely candidate for conversion to Christianity would be hard to find. Listen to Paul in Galatians 1:11-24:

> For I want you to know, brothers and sisters, that the gospel
> that was proclaimed by me is not of human origin; for I did

not receive it from a human source, nor was I taught it, but I received it through a revelation of Jesus Christ. You have heard, no doubt, of my earlier life in Judaism. I was violently persecuting the church of God and was trying to destroy it. I advanced in Judaism beyond many among my people of the same age, for I was far more zealous for the traditions of my ancestors. But when God, who had set me apart before I was born and called me through his grace, was pleased to reveal his Son to me, so that I might proclaim him among the Gentiles, I did not confer with any human being, not did I go up to Jerusalem to those who were already apostles before me, but I went away at once into Arabia and afterwards I returned to Damascus. Then after three years I did go up to Jerusalem to visit Cephas and stayed with him for fifteen days; but I did not see any other apostle except James the Lord's brother. In what I am writing you, before God, I do not lie! Then I went into the regions of Syria and Cilicia, and I was still unknown by sight to the churches of Judea that are in Christ; they only heard it said, "The one who formerly was persecuting us is now proclaiming the faith he once tried to destroy." And they glorified God because of me.

Three times the conversion experience of Paul is related by Luke in the Acts of the Apostles: first in 9:1-19, when reporting his conversion on the road to Damascus to persecute the Christians there; second in 22:3-16, where he shares the account of his conversion with the angry, Jewish crowd after his arrest in Jerusalem and rescue from the mob of Jews who sought his death; and finally in 26:9-18, where he addresses King Agrippa in self-defense after his arrest. It is clear that Paul understood by his conversion experience that he had seen the risen Christ in much the same way as the apostles had. In 1 Corinthians 9:1 he says, "Have I not seen Jesus our Lord?" and in 15:8 he equates his experience as identical to the appearances of Jesus to the disciples: "he appeared to me also." Questions can be raised about the nature of these appearances, but one thing is clear: Paul was completely convinced he had seen with his own eyes and heard with his own ears the crucified and risen Jesus that qualified and called him to be an apostolic witness. It created absolute conviction in this radical persecutor that this Jesus, whom he was opposing, was alive, and that the story of his life, death, and resurrection proclaimed by this fledging group of believers was true!

As I wrestled with the challenge of Schweitzer and McConnell to my faith, I confess what impressed me, as I read the New Testament as a whole, was that it they conveyed to me a fundamental affirmation of the resurrection. But it was especially the account of Paul and his conversion that conveyed to me what J. B. Phillips called the "Ring of Truth" — the sense of authenticity, the conviction of veracity, the assurance of its reality — that leaped from the New Testament pages. Something major happened, and nothing less than the bodily resurrection accounts for the existence of the church and the contents of this collected volume of letters and narratives. The New Testament preserved for the ages to follow the story and meaning of the church's beginning. The New Testament allows each generation of readers, as it were, to leap over the ages to the first century to read for themselves the firsthand testimony of the eyewitnesses, permanently preserved in written form for all future generations.

Daniel P. Fuller in his *Easter Faith and History*[5] proposes a fascinating interpretation of Luke–Acts, with Paul as a powerful apologetic for the truth of the resurrection. Luke prefaces his Gospel with this stated purpose:

> Since many have undertaken to set down an orderly account of the events that have been fulfilled among us, just as they were handed on to us by those who from the beginning

5. Grand Rapids: Eerdmans, 1965.

were eyewitnesses and servants of the word, I too decided, after investigating carefully from the very first, to write an orderly account for you, most excellent Theophilus, so that you may know the truth concerning the things about which you have been instructed. (Luke 1:1-4)

Having completed his Gospel, Luke continues writing the book of Acts, opening with these words: "In the first book, Theophilus, I wrote about all that Jesus did and taught from the beginning until the day when he was taken up to heaven, after giving instructions through the Holy Spirit to the apostles whom he had chosen" (Acts 1:1-2). Luke in Acts reports the ascension of Jesus and the outpouring of the Holy Spirit on Pentecost. He describes the growth and life of the early church in Jerusalem, as well as the growing opposition of the Jews and their persecution of Christians that reached a climax in the martyrdom of Stephen by stoning with Paul's approval. In the ninth chapter he narrates the amazing and dramatic story of the conversion of Paul, a principal opponent of the expanding church who was on his way to Damascus to continue his nefarious work. Then Luke proceeds to tell the gospel's crucially important and difficult break with Judaism through Peter, the chief of the apostles, to include Gentiles as uncircumcised members in the church. It is all invaluable data about the nascent church. But surprisingly, after that, the Acts no longer speaks of the twelve apostles and their ministry, but devotes the rest of Acts (chapters 13 to 28) to Paul's missionary activities in the Gentile world. It records his growing conflict with the authorities and concludes with his being taken as a prisoner to Rome to await judicial adjudication. The conversion story of Paul is repeated twice: to the angry mob of Jews in Jerusalem (22:6-11) and before Agrippa (26:12-18). Paul kept referring back to his conversion experience when he saw the resurrected Jesus. Why? Because the resurrection was of inestimable importance in Paul's defense of the gospel — just as it is today.

It was always a mystery to me that the book of Acts took the turn it did. It informs us only of Paul and his missionary tours, leaving us in the dark regarding the work of the rest of the apostles — including even Peter — as they spread the Word around the world until they met their ultimate fate. Daniel Fuller suggests that Luke, in writing the Gospel and the Acts, chose to be an apologist for the truth of the gospel, demonstrating the power of the risen Christ to convert the most unlikely candidate and transform him into an apostle who opened the doors of the church to the whole world. It is as if Luke is saying: do you want to know why we believe Christianity is true, Theophilus? See its truth in the Apostle Paul! In him you witness the reality and power of the risen Christ! The resurrection accounts for his conversion and missionary service. Paul appeals to his experience on the road to Damascus to explain his life first to the Jews and then to Agrippa and Felix, the political authorities. That Paul confirms the truth of the gospel is the theme of Luke's history; the transforming power of the risen Lord in the life of the Apostle Paul and his successful ministry in the Gentile world are credible grounds "on which we may know the certainty of the things [we] have been taught" (Luke 1:4). The Gospel of Luke and the Acts of the Apostles appear to be Luke's apologetics for the truth of Christianity itself.

It is primarily in the resurrection accounts of the four Gospels that we find the inconsistencies and apparent contradictions that puzzle us and that critics use to discredit belief in the resurrection. (I should note that some have claimed it is possible to reconcile all the accounts of the resurrection, as does Frank Morison in his popular book *Who Moved the Stone?*[6]) Basically the major discrepancies boil down to two problems concerning the appearances of the risen Christ: first, the *place* where they occurred — either in Jerusalem (Luke and John) or Galilee (Matthew and

6. Grand Rapids: Zondervan, 1977.

86

Mark) — and second, the *nature* of the appearances. Did Jesus appear as a resuscitated body, or in visions, or possibly in hallucinations as a glorified body? Puzzles also appear in the Gospel accounts regarding the number of women, angels, and appearances of Jesus at the empty tomb.

Whatever the problems in the New Testament witness to the resurrection, I find the argument of James Denney in his *Jesus and the Gospel*[7] a powerful rejoinder to the conclusion that the discrepancies in the Gospel accounts cast doubt on the fact of the resurrection itself:

> The real historical evidence for the resurrection is the fact that it was believed, preached, propagated and produced its fruit and effect in the new phenomenon of the Christian Church, long before any of our gospels was written. . . . Faith in the resurrection was not only prevalent but immensely powerful before any of our New Testament books was written. Not one of them would ever have been written but for that faith. It is not this or that in the New Testament — it is not the story of the empty tomb, or of the appearing of Jesus in Jerusalem or in Galilee — which is the primary evidence for the resurrection; it is the New Testament itself. . . . The evidence for the resurrection of Jesus is the existence of the Church in that extraordinary spiritual vitality which confronts us in the New Testament. . . . The existence of the Christian Church, the existence of the New Testament; these incomparable phenomena in human history are left without adequate or convincing explanation if the resurrection of Jesus be denied. (pp. 111-12)

Imagine for a moment that all the accounts were completely harmonious. Would not the critics then charge the disciples

7. London: Hodder and Stoughton, 1908.

with deliberate, organized deception? Human witness to most historical events is muddled and contradictory, all their elements difficult to reconcile as each witness reports what he or she has experienced from his or her perspective. In addition such data is always filtered through each mind that inevitably seeks to make a coherent whole from the data and impressions it receives from the senses. Think of all the confusing and conflicting reporting around the assassination of President John F. Kennedy in modern times, with all the advantages of the modern media and benefits of science and technology to determine what really happened! Even in March 2005, after forty-two years, *Reader's Digest* asked whether the murder of President Kennedy could finally be cracked with new technology. Were there two or three shots from the Texas School Book Depository behind the Presidential motorcade, or was there a shot from someone else on the grassy knoll ahead? Did Lee Harvey Oswald act alone? Did the fact that he spent time in Communist Russia and had connections with Cuba contribute to his assassinating crime? Or were there gangster connections with organized crime that involved Oswald and that incited Jack Ruby to murder him two days after his arrest to avoid exposure of such connections? There are many questions that in the minds of many people remain unanswered, but the end result is not that President Kennedy was not in fact assassinated. In the same way, the inconsistencies and contradictions in the stories of the resurrection do not prove that Jesus did not rise from the dead. I believe, in fact, that the diversity in the gospel testimony argues for its authenticity. The conflicting accounts arise precisely because there was an event, the resurrection, about which conflicting stories could arise.

Even the liberal Reginald H. Fuller, at the conclusion of his study *The Formation of the Resurrection Narratives*,[8] writes,

8. New York: Macmillan, 1971.

We began this work by characterizing the difficulties which the resurrection narratives create for modern man. Many of these difficulties arise from the inconsistencies between the different versions of the Easter stories in the Gospels. It seemed hopeless to try and reconstruct what happened, and that basic uncertainty threatened to undermine the whole foundation of the Christian faith.

A study of the resurrection narratives with the modern methods of tradition and redaction criticism enables us to explain the inconsistencies and contradictions. They have nothing to do with the primary uncertainty about the resurrection faith. Rather they represent varying attempts to give that faith expression. At the very earliest stage in the tradition, the resurrection events were not related: rather, the resurrection was proclaimed. "God raised Jesus from the dead." This proclamation was couched in the language of Jewish apocalyptic, which had hoped for the day when the elect would be raised out of their graves and enter into an entirely new mode of existence. What the apocalyptic hope had anticipated has now been fulfilled in the case of a single individual, Jesus of Nazareth, whose resurrection, however, was to be decisive for the subsequent raising of the dead in the very near future. (pp. 168-69)

The Common Catechism[9] is an ecumenical work, drawing not only on the resources of many nations, but also on all major Western Christian traditions. Written by an international team of forty Protestant and Roman Catholic theologians, it addresses Jesus' resurrection and the Easter faith:

The proclamation of Jesus' resurrection is not an additional, and essentially superfluous, appendage to the story of Jesus

9. Johannes Feiner, *The Common Catechism: A Book of Christian Faith* (New York: Seabury Press, 1975).

and the gospels. It is more an expression of how the primitive community, and with them the writers of the gospels, saw their relation to Jesus of Nazareth "after Easter." For them the person and work of Jesus were in no way finished by the cross; they had brought into being a new movement of development. This led to the formation of a community of salvation, the Church, characterized by faith in Jesus as the Messiah. It led to the formulation and proclamation of a gospel in which the crucified Messiah Jesus was preached as the "Son of God" who had been raised from the dead, as "Lord" and "redeemer," as the saving act of God. It led to the mission to the nations, to liberation from the Jewish religion of law. In short, it began everything which later led to Christianity's becoming a "world religion," a faith directed to all nations.

According to the evidence of the New Testament documents, the initial event which started off all these others, above all the formation of the community and the public preaching of Jesus as the Messiah, is very closely connected with what is described by the phrase "the resurrection of Jesus." However one may interpret the Easter faith of the primitive Church, it is impossible to avoid the problem of this "initial event," as it may be called for the moment. This problem is the fact that after Good Friday there was a new start for the disciples of Jesus, a new start which requires a satisfactory explanation. . . .

It is much more difficult to give a satisfactory explanation for the fact that Jesus of Nazareth himself, who had been crucified, now became the central content of the gospel which began to be preached. The New Testament does not say that Jesus' message was right in spite of Good Friday, but that *Good Friday itself has become the main theme of faith, through its connexion with the claim that Jesus was raised from the dead by God.* (pp. 162-64)

It is of course possible within the Christian community to have differing opinions as to how the biblical testimony on the resurrection is to be understood. When attending a summer session at Union Theological Seminary in New York, I had the unique privilege of several visits with Donald Baillie, author of the famed and now classic book, *God Was in Christ.*[10] I knew Dr. Baillie to be a very devout Christian; going to his class was like going to church — he opened and closed the sessions with beautiful prayers. I knew he affirmed the resurrection but heard he did not believe the tomb was empty. On one of our visits I asked him if he did not accept the bodily resurrection of Jesus and the empty tomb because it was considered scientifically impossible. He immediately responded, "Oh no, science has nothing to say about it," affirming that the question was outside the jurisdiction of science. His questioning of the bodily resurrection, he said, arose out of St. Paul's statement that it was raised a "spiritual body" in 1 Corinthians 15. For him it was not a question of whether the resurrection happened, but what the nature of the happening was as reported in the Scriptures. The same is true for G. W. H. Lampe who considers the story of the empty tomb as myth rather than as literal history, and profoundly significant as myth.

But I believe we cannot affirm the resurrection of Jesus apart from his earthly body. Does not the concept of resurrection require some kind of continuity with the physical body? Does not the Apostle Paul's discussion of the resurrection body in 1 Corinthians 15:35-49 assume continuity between a seed that is planted and the plant that grows from it? These are the questions I should have addressed to Dr. Baillie, but did not. These are the kind of problems I had to address in my search for a reasonable Christian faith. But they are questions within the circle of believers about which there can be differences of opinion without casting doubt on the fact of the resurrection, though they may raise

10. New York: C. Scribner's Sons, 1948.

pertinent questions about the inspiration and inerrancy of the Scriptures.

The scriptural data on the nature of the resurrected body is confusing to our minds. It appears to be much like a resuscitated body when Jesus asks doubting Thomas to "put your finger here; see my hands. Reach out your hand and put it in my side" (John 20:27). Yet the body could appear and reappear through closed doors as we read in John 20:26: "Though the doors were locked, Jesus came and stood among them." I remember when I was eleven or twelve our saintly old pastor in catechism class asking if there was anything in heaven that had been made on earth. That seemed improbable to us until the pastor pointed out the wounds in Jesus' hands and side must be there, because his resurrection body still bore those wounds according to the biblical account. The pastor believed they are an eternal witness to the price our Lord paid to redeem us from our sins.

The resurrected body was both unrecognizable and recognizable, as in John 21, when Jesus appeared on the shore, and in Luke 24 where the disciples thought they saw a ghost (v. 33), and the men on the road to Emmaus did not recognize him until he broke the bread at supper (v. 31). And in Matthew 28, apparently at the time of his ascension, we are told when the eleven disciples saw Jesus they worshiped him "but some doubted" (v. 17). Apparently the appearance of Jesus was sufficiently different to arouse doubt in the minds of some. These conflicting stories of the appearances of Jesus are frequently used to question the reality of the resurrection, but who is to say what the nature of the resurrected body is and what its potentials are to adapt to the occasions in which the risen Jesus appeared? Christians believe it was a foretaste of the renewed creation, about which we know too little to make judgments in the light of this present world. The Gospel accounts only illustrate the mysteries that surround the world to come as they are revealed in the resurrected Jesus.

It is important to remember that the Gospels were written decades after the resurrection event and collected from diverse apostolic sources. Luke reports that "many have undertaken to draw up an account of the things that have been fulfilled among us, just as they were handed down to us by those who from the first were eyewitnesses and servants of the word" (1:1, 2). The writers of Matthew, Mark, Luke, and John were all closely associated with the apostles on their missionary journeys. They heard the various apostles recall their memories of the events they experienced, the miracles they witnessed, the teaching of Jesus they memorized after the fashion of students taught by rabbis in those ancient days, their ignominious cowardice at the end of Jesus' life, and then the amazing event of the resurrection after three days. Each apostle, with slight differences of memory, addressed different audiences, under different conditions, with different applications, and in turn the authors of the Gospels heard the apostles, each with the understanding of his own individual mind and memory. Isn't it to be expected that their Gospel presentations would embody differences that in the sum total amount to only minor differences — and that their differences are to be expected if the resurrection really happened?

It is not my intention to deal with the particulars of all the biblical evidence on the resurrection. The best available work on the subject is N. T. Wright's *The Resurrection of the Son of God.*[11] I was privileged to hear his series of lectures on the resurrection at Union Theological Seminary in Richmond, Virginia, in January 2002. Dr. Wright is firmly committed to the bodily resurrection of Jesus Christ:

> The question that must be faced is whether the explanation
> of the data which the early Christians themselves gave, that
> Jesus really was risen from the dead 'explains the aggregate'
> of the evidence better than those sophisticated skepticisms.
> My claim is that it does.

11. Minneapolis: Augsburg Fortress, 2003.

The claim can be stated once more in terms of necessary and sufficient conditions. The actual bodily resurrection of Jesus (not a mere resuscitation, but a transforming revivification) clearly provides a sufficient condition of the tomb being empty and the 'meetings' taking place. Nobody is likely to doubt that. Once grant that Jesus really was raised, and all the pieces of the historical jigsaw puzzle of early Christianity fall into place. My claim is stronger: that the bodily resurrection provides a necessary condition for these things; in other words, that no other explanation could or would do. All the efforts to find alternative explanations fail, and they were bound to do so. . . .

Historical argument alone cannot force anyone to believe that Jesus was raised from the dead; but historical argument is remarkably good at clearing away the undergrowth behind which skepticisms of various sorts have been hiding. *The proposal that Jesus was bodily raised from the dead possesses unrivalled power to explain the historical data at the heart of early Christianity.* (pp. 717-18; italics mine)

It is of course impossible to prove the resurrection with mathematical certainty, as it is for most historical events. I am convinced, however, as Dr. Wright states, that it is most reasonable from the accumulated evidence to believe that the resurrection was an event in history at a specific time and place.

To believe in the resurrection is to believe a miracle occurred. A miracle as the dictionary describes it is "an event or action that apparently contradicts known scientific laws and is hence thought to be due to supernatural causes, especially to an act of God." The Scriptures repeatedly teach that "God . . . raised Christ from the dead" (1 Corinthians 15:15). According to Wright, it is far more reasonable to believe the miracle of the resurrection than any naturalistic explanation — unless, of course, one is so blinded by dogmatic naturalism that miracles simply never happen.

The reality of a miracle in the setting of the crucifixion of Jesus can be explained only by the action of God above and beyond the naturalistic potentials in the universe. The cosmological and teleological arguments are rooted in nature. The resurrection is powerful evidence for God's existence in human history.

But having revealed himself in this way, why does God so often hide himself? This is a refrain in the Scriptures, frequently echoed by Christians themselves when they fear their loneliness and need in the universe. Why doesn't God reveal himself in answer to our prayers in times of despair and helplessness? For God to do so would then prove his existence in a way that would vitiate his purposes with us. His purpose with us is to reveal himself in a way that depends upon a response of trust, which human beings are free to withhold if they so desire; he does not violate human independence. God does not compel trust by exhibiting undeniable evidence of his power in any form. But both in the works of nature and in the revelation contained in the Bible he offers us opportunities for accepting or rejecting him.

Alasdair C. MacIntyre, in his *Difficulties in Christian Belief,*[12] writes:

> The paradigm case, that case which shows most clearly what is essentially involved, of God's dealings with men, is his dealing with them in the person of Jesus Christ. . . . [W]hen he comes to afford St. Thomas, the apostle, proof of the Resurrection, what is logically important is that if Thomas were deceived by the visual appearance of Christ, he might after all have been equally deceived in touching his hands and his side. Both vision and touch might have been hallucinatory. When Thomas fell before Christ saying "My Lord and my God," he was not choosing to trust rather than to prove Christ; he was showing his consciousness of the fact that the

12. London: SCM Press, 1959.

only issue before him was to trust or not to trust. There could have been no proof offered which would not have been such that he could not have found good reason for rejecting it if he so desired. To ask for proof is to put oneself outside the only attitude in which it is possible to confront God; and therefore refusing to believe because one cannot have proofs is a simple missing of the point. (pp. 83-84)

At the beginning of this chapter I summarized the impact of the church in the world and its tremendous influence in society. I find it implausible that it resulted from the figments of Peter's mind. As I am writing this, the news has been dominated by the death of Pope John Paul II and the election of Pope Benedict XVI. A scene that moved me deeply was at the funeral of John Paul, in the open square before the Cathedral of St. Peter in Rome. His body lay in a simple wooden box in the center of the plaza before the cathedral, surrounded by the huge mass of mourners that included leaders of the free world paying their tribute, the red-cloaked Cardinals, the white-cloaked bishops and priests, the mass of people overflowing the square, all before the magnificent splendor of St. Peter's Cathedral. And near the head of the pope's body stood a simple wooden crucifix to remind the world it all began in history with the crucifixion and death of Jesus, a condemned criminal two thousand years ago on a hilltop outside the city gates of Jerusalem. What an unlikely story! Could anything other than a miracle put those two facts together? What could possibly explain that scene other than the resurrection? Christianity itself, originating in history under conditions of the greatest difficulty, is powerful evidence for the resurrection!

We have already noted in Chapter Two that Karl Barth adopted the resurrection of Christ as the starting point of his theology. He often gave as his reason for doing so that it was from the perspective of the resurrection that the whole of the New Testament presentation of Christ is focused. The resurrection discloses the existence of another world, the world of God. The resurrection provides powerful evidence for the reality of a supernatural, personal God to account for its occurrence. It most effectively illumines human existence by revealing the nature, character, and purposes of God through the revelation of himself in Jesus Christ. "Anyone who has seen me has seen the Father" (John 14:9). Barth authored fourteen hefty volumes of *Church Dogmatics*[13] and numerous other books on theology on the basis of that revelatory standpoint.

Listen to Daniel Jenkins in his little book *Believing in God:*[14]

It is essential that we see how the whole question concerning the reality of the Christian God gathers to a head in the cross and resurrection of Christ. Unless we do, the reality of God becomes a matter of interesting speculation rather than one that genuinely determines human destiny. Nowhere is that reality of God and the covenant he made with Israel put to the test more searchingly than in these tremendous events. All the threats to meaning in human life are gathered up in the expiring cry of Jesus as he hangs on the cross, "My God, my God, why hast thou forsaken me?" And all the hopes of the fulfillment of true life in eternity go with his lifeless body into the tomb. If Jesus lived and died in vain, the Christian God does not exist.

It was out of the conviction that God in Jesus Christ had proved himself stronger than the cross and the tomb, that the Christian faith was born. The evidence for this conviction is given in the resurrection experience, which was the supreme vindication of the faith of Jesus. That is why Easter has always been recognized as the most distinctive festival

13. Edinburgh: T&T Clark, 1956-1975.
14. Philadelphia: Westminster Press, 1956.

of the Church's life and why, in periods of its clear vision, the Church as always insisted that belief in the Christian God depends on knowledge of the risen Christ. (pp. 45-46)

To quote Jenkins again:

At the heart of Christian teaching about God lies this testimony, first made in the Scriptures and confirmed in the experience of an innumerable company of believers in every age since the first: that the ultimate Power in the whole universe, on whom all else depends, has made himself known uniquely in Jesus Christ as a just and loving Father, who bears the consequences of human rebellion against him and imparts his own reconciling and renewing life to man, and who has promised to be with his children until the end of all things. (p. 52)

There is a fundamental difference between naturalism's view of reality and the Christian view, as we saw in Chapter Three. Naturalism views the universe as nature: forms of materialism. It has no room for either a divine or human person, nor does it find any significance in human history. A person is only a byproduct of the evolutionary process, so that when she dies her mind no longer exists. It was this bleak view of existentialism against which Sartre rebelled when near the close of his life he said, "I do not feel that I am the product of chance, a speck of dust in the universe, but someone expected, prepared, prefigured. In short, a being whom only a Creator could put here, and this idea of a creating hand refers to God."[15] Descartes taught us that the most basic certainty is our existence: "I doubt, therefore I know I exist." And not only I, but others as well, and the universe in which we live. Thus the most basic and fundamental reality in the universe is

15. *The National Review,* June 11, 1982, p. 677.

the mind. God is a Spirit; he is the Divine Mind, the Creator of the universe. The resurrection two thousand years ago is a remarkably powerful evidence of God's reality.

Is it not reasonable to hypothesize from the existence of our minds to the existence of a Divine Mind that created the order and complexity of the universe, and integrated all of its parts to compose a marvelously unified and purposeful whole? In fact, is it not unreasonable to suppose that the only intelligent beings in the universe are on this earth? Is their presence here little more than an accident of existence with no permanent meaning in the totality of the universe? Is not the human mind the highest and most mysterious form of creation? Is it not endowed with the capacity "to think God's thoughts after him"? Is it not reasonable to expect to discover a Divine Mind that infuses the totality of the universe with his wisdom and power and divine purpose? As we noted in Chapter Three, Alfred N. Whitehead found it necessary to structure "God" into his metaphysics — however difficult it may be to understand his concept of God.[16] Although Whitehead's view of God differs from the God confessed in the Christian faith, the fact that he needed a "God" at all, beyond nature, to explain his concept of the universe is a telling blow to naturalism. Is it any wonder that the atheists objected so strenuously to Whitehead's God? And that they do the same thing with the "Intelligent Design" theory today?

Historically we know that Jesus died on the cross. Historically, we know that within Jerusalem shortly afterwards, a church in his name was formed by his disciples. They were a defeated group at the time of Jesus' arrest, but after a few weeks were boldly proclaiming his resurrection in the very presence of the powerful authorities who had been responsible for his condemnation and

---

16. George F. Thomas in his *Religious Philosophies of the West* (New York: Charles Scribner's Sons, 1965) devotes twenty-four pages to explain Whitehead's concept of God!

death. What explains their startling message? What explains their new boldness? What explains their rapid growth and remarkable success? Their answer: the resurrection of Jesus and his continuing presence after Pentecost in the Holy Spirit. The expanding church two thousand years later continues proclaiming that same consistent message of the living Christ who arose on the first Easter.

Is it not patently absurd to regard our human minds as the highest form of life amid the galaxies of universes? Consider: we inhabit one small planet that swirls around one small star among uncounted others. We scan the outer recesses of space and scope the minutest structures of the atom. Our life span is less than one century in the eons of time. Isn't it far more reasonable to believe there is a Divine Mind whose thoughts we dimly perceive in nature and in history and who has visited our planet in Jesus Christ to astonish us with his amazing grace? Is not the Christian worldview more meaningful when the resurrection of Jesus sheds the light of God on where we came from, why we are here, and where we are going? In the panorama of human existence all around us, the resurrection gives meaning, purpose, and hope that is uniquely called the "good news" of God.

Some may hasten to object and cite the horrors of nature in rebuttal: hurricanes, tornadoes, earthquakes, floods, fires, and the like. The existence of such catastrophes causes problems that Christians must wrestle with, but catastrophes do not negate the positive presence of God's intelligent creation. In fact there are many questions that can be raised which we must confront — questions that arise in the Bible itself, questions about the dark side to the story of the church, the problem of suffering, the mystery of continuing evil, the delay of Christ's return, the presence of other religions, the difficulty of evangelism. It is not given to us to know all the ways of God with man, but these difficult mysteries of our existence do not negate what we do know. The Apostle Paul, in tracing out the ways of God, is moved to a doxology of praise: "O the depth of the riches of the wisdom and knowledge of God! How unsearchable his judgments, and his paths beyond tracing out! 'Who has known the mind of the Lord?'" (Romans 11:33, 34).

Alasdair MacIntyre, author of *Difficulties in Christian Belief,* converted to Christianity as an adult, but went on to repudiate the Christian faith. When asked why he had renounced Christianity, it was not, he said, because of intellectual difficulties with the faith, which he professed, for it seemed the best of all worldviews, but because it meant nothing — it was meaningless! Later on, however, he returned to Christianity, and taught philosophy at Notre Dame. I have often wondered what it was that convinced MacIntyre that the Christian faith *did* make a difference that enabled him to return to his commitment. How do people become believers? Ultimately there is the mystery of the Holy Spirit at work deep in the recesses of every human heart.

Becoming a believer has a useful parallel in the person-to-person relationship of marriage. For some "falling in love" is almost instantaneous; for others it comes through a difficult, prolonged courtship of agonizing uncertainty. I know of one instance in which the uncertain party sought psychological help that proved effective for a long and rewarding marriage. Some couples simply grow in quiet affection until it is natural for them to pledge their lives to each other. Others make a leap of faith that may or may not lead to a happy union. So our commitment to Christ comes in a variety of ways, and finally involves a leap of faith — a leap that is reasonable to take in view of its unrivalled power to explain the historical data at the heart of early Christianity. But faith is always present in interpersonal relations — as is doubt.

MANY OF US affirm our faith in Christ Jesus with the prayer, "help my unbelief." I hope that my personal struggles, centering in the resurrection, may help you strengthen your faith in the gospel of our Lord's living presence. Luke Timothy Johnson, in his *The Real Jesus,* says:[17]

> Christian faith is directed to a living person. The "real Jesus" for Christian faith is the resurrected Jesus, him "whom God has made both Lord and Christ" (Acts 2:36) . . . [T]he *real Jesus* for Christian faith is not simply a figure of the past but very much and above all a figure of the present, a figure, indeed, who defines the believer's present by his presence. . . .
>
> The situation with the Christian's memory of Jesus is not like that of a long-ago lover who died and whose short time with us is treasured. The situation, rather, is like that of a lover who continues to live with the beloved in a growing and maturing relationship. In such a situation, the memory of the past is constantly affected by the continuing experience of the other in the present. For me (I am sure, for my wife), the issue of where my wife and I had our first date, or realized we were in love, or even made our vows, is of much less significance to each of us than the issue of whether our love is alive and powerfully real now, in the present. Moreover, even though the love shown me by my wife is experienced as continuous with that she showed me in the early years of our relationship, in no way do I find that love *dependent* on the right interpretation of those earlier experiences. Our relationship is confirmed or disconfirmed not by settling the issue of who we were back then but by engaging the issue of who we will be together now. So also is the Church's memory of Jesus constantly affected by his continuous and powerful presence and confirmed or disconfirmed by the reality of his presence. (pp. 141-43)

If it is true, as T. S. Matthew wrote, that humans are only really concerned about "news of life and death," it is because we fear

17. San Francisco: Harper, 1996.

death; it is the ultimate enemy. But we are not without hope. Listen to the Apostle Paul in 1 Corinthians 15:12-20:

> But if it is preached that Christ has been raised from the dead, how can some of you say that there is no resurrection of the dead? If there is no resurrection of the dead, then not even Christ has been raised. And if Christ has not been raised, our preaching is useless and so is your faith. More than that, we are then found to be false witnesses about God, for we have testified about God that he raised Christ from the dead. But he did not raise him if in fact the dead are not raised. For if the dead are nor raised, then Christ has not been raised either. And if Christ has not been raised, your faith his futile; you are still in your sins. . . . If only for this life we have hope in Christ, we are to be pitied more than all men. But Christ has indeed been raised from the dead, the firstfruits of those who have fallen asleep.

When the gospel of the risen Lord was first proclaimed, it was especially true for the suffering slaves and downtrodden masses of the ancient world for whom this life was unimaginably miserable, totally meaningless, and tragically hopeless. But the resurrection has provided a source of hope for countless millions ever since. Sholem Asch, in his *The Apostle*,[18] understood this. He tells the powerful and moving story of a wretched, miserable slave woman in Corinth:

> In the mephitic underground world of the bronze foundries, among the red flicker of the caldrons, the word spread quickly that there had arisen in the world an offer of redemption and reparation; and the story was told of a house of God the doors of which were open, beyond the grave, for

18. New York: Putnam's Sons, 1943, pp. 435-36.

all the righteous. On the threshold of the house of God stood
the Man-God who had prepared the portion of the righteous. . . . This Man-God had lived on earth, and he had suf-
fered like themselves, he had died as they did: and now he
stood on the threshold, beyond the grave. He would receive
them, wipe away their tears, comfort them for their sufferings, and would reward the good according to their good-
ness and the wicked according to their wickedness. And no
matter how low they were sunk in slavery here, in the lord,
the Man-God, they were free.

Above ground, among the polishers and hammerers, a
woman slave sat with her children. On her knees she held a
bronze vase, on which she was working. Part of the process
intended to bring out the special luster of Corinthian vases
demanded that the women polish the metal against their
own skins; thus, it was believed, the oils of the human body
would soften the color of the bronze. The vase which the
woman was polishing with her flesh was a particularly precious work of art, destined for one of the richest customers
of the bronze-master. It had the form of a young girl's body,
supple and curved, with a long slender neck, and an opening
that suggested soft parting lips. Near the mother, who sat
mechanically rubbing the vase against her hips, was a child,
a girl, perhaps six years of age. But the face of the little one
scarcely resembled the face of a human being. From head to
foot the child was covered with sores. Her eyes were closed
by heavy blisters so that she could barely see. In her bony little hands she held a bronze cup, part of the set which be-
longed to the vase, and with the last remnants of her
strength she, in imitation of her mother, was polishing the
metal against her flesh. But there was neither warmth nor
softness in the child's body; all that it exuded was a yellow-
ish matter mixed with blood, which stained the surface of
the cup. An overseer had marked this, and he passed the

word to one of the half-naked slaves who carried whips. A brutal hand was laid on the child. The mother half rose, and was flung back by the flick of the lash. She turned, with a choked cry, to the woman at the next block.

"Tell me, quickly, what was his name — the one who waits on the other side — the one whose name was given us by Lucius — quick — his name!"

"Jesus Christ."

"Jesus Christ, take my child unto thee!"

READERS WILL likely be surprised by the unlikely setting that inspired me to write this book: it was, of all things, the Radio City Christmas Spectacular of December 2002 in New York City. It included "The Living Nativity" scene celebrating the birth of Jesus. As a live camel and two donkeys paraded across the mammoth stage, a rich voice intoned *One Solitary Life*. I was deeply moved by this pageantry in a secular setting that must have evoked from at least some in the audience the question of who this Jesus really was:

He was born in an obscure village, the child of a peasant woman. He grew up in another obscure village, where He worked in a carpenter shop until he was thirty. Then for three years He was an itinerant preacher. He never had a family or owned a home. He never set foot inside a big city. He never traveled two hundred miles from the place He was born. He never wrote a book or held an office. He did none of the things that usually accompany greatness.

While He was still a young man, the tide of popular opinion turned against Him. His friends deserted Him. He was turned over to his enemies, and went through the mockery of a trial. He was nailed to a cross between two thieves. While He was dying, His executioners gambled for the only piece of property He had — His coat. When He was dead, He was taken down and laid in a borrowed grave.

Over two thousand years have passed, and today He is the central figure for much of the human race. All the armies that ever marched and all the navies that ever sailed and the parliaments that ever sat and all the kings that ever reigned, put together, have not affected the life of man upon the earth as powerfully as this "One Solitary Life."

When the scene ended I wanted to proclaim to the standing, applauding audience: "What accounts for this 'One Solitary Life,' this amazing life of Jesus? It is Easter! It is his resurrection!"

Index of Names

INDEX OF NAMES

Küng, Hans, 29

Ladd, George E., 35
Lampe, G. W. H., 75, 76, 77, 91
Lapide, Pinchas, 53
Latourette, Kenneth Scott, 71
Lewis, C. S., 4, 33
Lewis, Edwin, 13, 14
Ludemann, Gerd, 64
Luther, Martin, 13

Machen, J. Gresham, 15
MacKinnon, D. W., 76, 78
Marty, Martin, 72
Matthew, T. S., 39, 77, 102
McConnell, S. D., 4, 5, 6, 7, 9, 10, 11, 13, 25, 26, 84
MacIntyre, Alasdair D., 33, 95, 101
Moltmann, Jürgen, 30
Morison, Frank, 86

Niebuhr, Reinhold, 14, 55, 69
Noll, Mark, 43

Pannenberg, Wolfhart, 67
Pascal, Blaise, 49
Pauck, Wilhelm, 14
Phillips, J. B., 84
Picht, Werner, 4, 7
Pittenger, Norman, 54
Plantinga, Alvin, 65
Pope Benedict XVI, 96
Pope John Paul II, 96

Read, Harris, 12
Reimarus, Hermann S., 64
Ritschl, Albrecht, 37
Robinson, James M., 16
Robinson, John A. T., 15

Rolston, Holmes, 37
Russell, Bertrand, 68

Sagan, Carl, 34
Sartre, Jean Paul, 57, 58, 98
Schillebeeckx, Edward, 65, 66
Schleiermacher, Friedrich, 37
Schweitzer, Albert, 1, 2, 3, 4, 7, 9, 10, 11, 12, 13, 18, 25, 26, 37, 66, 68, 76, 84
Smart, James D., 31
Smedes, Lewis, 27, 38
Smith, Huston, 40
Smith, Morton, 64
Stauffer, Ethelbert, 63
Stewart, James S., 15, 41
Stob, Henry, 13, 21
Strauss, David, 37

Tenney, Merrill C., 59
Thiering, Barbara, 64
Thomas, George F., 48, 99
Tillich, Paul, 14
Tombaugh, Clyde W., 20
Torrance, Thomas F., 15, 23, 38
Troeltsch, Ernst, 37

Van Buren, Paul M., 51, 53, 65
Van Paassen, Pierre, 65
Victor, Pierre, 58
Vitz, Paul C., 47

Wells, G. A., 64
Whale, John S., 14, 15
Whitehead, Alfred North, 16, 56, 99
Wieman, Henry Nelson, 55, 56
Will, George F., 49
Wright, N. T., 65, 93, 94